Is There a SPEECH Inside You?

About the Author

Don Aslett's approach to public speaking is tried and true — with over 8,000 public speeches under his belt, it should be! He began his speaking career as a "janitor with a message," based on his cleaning expertise established by his best-selling book, *Is There Life After Housework?*, and his conviction that pride in your work is the true key to success in any endeavor. From speeches for the world's largest corporations to graduation ceremonies, and everything in between, Don's done it all. In his inspirational manner, he shares his trials and tribulations, as well as his exhilaration and excitement, with readers around the world.

In addition to the best-seller, *Is There Life After House-work?*, Don Aslett is the author of *Do I Dust or Vacuum First?*, *Clutter's Last Stand*, *Who Says It's a Woman's Job to Clean?*, *Pet Clean-Up Made Easy*, and *Make Your House Do the Housework* (with Laura Aslett Simons).

Is There a
SPEECH
Inside You?

Don Aslett

92 91 90 89 88   5 4 3 2 1

Library of Congress Cataloging-in-Publication Data

Aslett, Don, 1935-
  Is there a speech inside you? / Don Aslett.
    p.   cm.
  ISBN 0-89879-351-0
  1. Public speaking. I. Title.
  PN4121.A226   1989
  808.51—dc20

Cincinnati, Ohio

First published in Great Britain in 1988 by Exley Publications Ltd.

92 91 90 89 88 5 4 3 2 1

Library of Congress Cataloging-in-Publication Data

Aslett, Don, 1935-
      Is there a speech inside you? /Don Aslett.
        p. cm.
        ISBN 0-89879-361-0
        1.Public speaking. I. Title
PN4121.A726 1989
808.5'1-dc20

89-5764
CIP

Illustrations by David Lock

Contents

*Fainting – Dry throat – Nobody comes – Too
many people come – You go blank – Foot-in-
mouth mistakes*

Introduction

Who is Don Aslett and why does he think he knows anything about public speaking?

Don Aslett's impressive record of over 8,000 public speeches lends credibility to his advice and directions for how you can become a professional speaker. From addresses to the world's largest corporations to graduations, from hilarious stage entertainments to funerals, from national TV and radio appearances to conventions, seminars, and training sessions, from sermons from the pulpit to debates on the legislative floor, from serving as a tour guide to coaching people to talk, Don has done it successfully – hundreds of times throughout the U.S. and overseas. His clients constantly say he's the best they've ever heard. As perhaps befits a man whose original professional credits were as a farmer and janitor, Don brings a very down-to-earth and refreshing approach to speaking in *Is There a Speech Inside You?* (His writing skills match his speaking skills, as you know if you've ever read one of his best-selling books.) Don, Chairman of the Board of one of America's most successful cleaning firms, owns several businesses. He is married and has six children and he divides his time between the mountains of Idaho and the mountains of Hawaii.

Chapter One

Kill me ... but don't ask me to get up and speak

The purpose of this book is to dramatically improve the attitude of the 90% of us who fear we can't make a public speech anytime, anywhere to anyone.

As one person put it, "I even get nervous and sweaty when they ask me to give a silent prayer!" On the other side of town, a top executive was considering giving up work rather than face tomorrow and the assignment of conducting seventy people through a one-hour business forum.

More people are afraid of speaking in public than are afraid of flying, or even loneliness. The average person has hundreds of opportunities to speak, and devises hundreds of ways to avoid that firing squad of audience eyeballs.

If you can talk, you can speak

This looming sentence of doom has made you miserable, ineffective and unproductive. In your previous attempts (if any) to speak in public, the only clue the listeners got that you were trying to communicate was that your lips were moving. Yet in your personal everyday life, speaking is the easiest, most natural, rewarding experience you know. Speaking publicly (which is only conversation on a bigger scale) is actually easier and more fun and I guarantee it will be the most rewarding experience of your life.

13

MY PROMISE: *Good public speaking can be learned in hours. If you'll take a couple of hours to read this book, the public won't let you stop.*

Once you master the simple basics of speaking as I explain them in these pages, you'll be a professional, and better than 80% of the speakers you see and hear today!

Why should you speak?

Because you as an individual are the most valuable resource on the earth. When you say, express, project something meaningful, your business, your community, and even your own life is immediately the better for it.

Because you've always wanted to. You have lots of feelings and opinions you'd like to make known to the rest of us and you'd love to be a dynamic speaker.

Because very few others can or will speak up and many of those who do are chloroform on the hoof. You don't just want to be an onlooker, a follower, a sheep – and you're not. How many good speeches have you heard lately? Too few. That platform, that speaker's stand needs you.

Because you can also enhance your job, your organization, company, school, church. Why should those organizations have to go to outsiders, to professionals, when you have within you the material and the wisdom to do much better? How can you sell, manage, or lead if you can't speak or teach?

Because there are thousands of people, organizations and nations who need and want to hear what you have to say, and they'll even pay you for it.

It's you that will gain

There are personal rewards for becoming a dynamic speaker and communicator. You gain:

★ **Poise**

Along with confidence and self esteem. A sense of self-worth surrounds you when you present yourself and your material well.

★ **Power**

The skill and ability to convince and influence is one of the greatest powers on earth. This is true in the home and in business.

★ **Position**

When you add this resource, this dimension to your talents and abilities, you become more valuable – promotions, opportunities, and advancement follow. And you may even get paid more!

★ **Achievement**

Changing and influencing others' lives to the good is a worthwhile achievement and powerful, eloquent speech is one of the best ways to accomplish this.

Why speak up?

The businessman stopped in a pet shop during his lunch hour to browse and wound up paying a fortune for a parrot that spoke five languages. The shop delivered the bird to his home that afternoon.

He rushed into the house after work, eager to impress his wife with his acquisition. He asked if the bird had been delivered.

"Yes, it's here" she answered. "In the oven."

"In the oven?" the husband roared. "Why that bird cost a fortune and knew five different languages."

"Well," said the wife calmly, "why didn't he speak up?"

There is hardly a position in life these days where we can be excused from or truly dodge the responsibility of speaking up, of addressing the group, or "performing," whether we're part of a white collar brain trust or running a road crew. The days of the invisible, anonymous, silent worker, citizen, student, or business executive are gone!

Only a few who do the talking, presenting, and public appearances in business, school and church meetings do it well. The rest don't speak well or don't speak at all. Why should we let a small percentage of us do all the talking when anyone can speak dynamically?

Start it all off by saying YES!

Say "YES, I'll do it." Not "Yes, I'll try." – **"Yes, I'll do it!"**

Don't put it off like you did last time, and the time before that. Commit yourself to it now: You will accept any and all oral presentations or talking in front of a group that's suggested to you.

Where should you speak?

This is the age of the stage ... everywhere you go, you have an audience.

Business: Businesses are literally starving for people who can stand up and tell the company story well. They're full of well-educated, seasoned managers and sage employees whose finest and only good presentations are given at coffee breaks. They have all kinds of well-qualified, progressive people who boil with ability and potential, but because they can't effectively share it with others in public, it's of no value to the company. The opportunities for public speaking in a

company are numerous, but shamefully, the company often has to turn to a tape recorder to convey the message. It's probably about one-quarter as effective as you would be in person. If you can't think of any situation that calls for speaking in your business, how about:

- Conventions
- New product presentations
- Oral reports
- Meetings
- Awards presentations
- Plant or office tours
- Sales presentations
- Business proposals

- Introductions
- Customer demonstrations
- Committee representation
- Announcements or reports
- Prayers
- Occasions that call for defence of beliefs, principles, courses of action or points of view
- At least fifty more....

Community: Like most people, you are (and always have been) full of opinions as to what's wrong and what could be better. The trouble is, only your close friends and family have heard your solutions. You have every right to these opinions and in a democracy, you actually have an obligation to your community and country to take part in the "debate." If you aren't heard, it'll only be your fault. Communities need voices and leaders, and if the good thinkers can't talk to the community strongly, convincingly, spontaneously, they'll be ignored and everyone will be the poorer for it.

Schools are a prime example. I've served on school boards and watched hundreds of parents and others come to meetings to express their needs and feelings. These people had good causes, logical ideas, and important information, but because they lacked speaking technique most of them didn't have a chance of getting their message across.

There are hundreds of community opportunities for public speaking – here are a few situations in which good speaking

16

ability can enrich your life and the lives of others:

- School meetings
- Civic and political gatherings
- Clubs
- Scout meetings
- Weddings
- Youth camps
- Summer camp events
- Banquets
- Rallies
- Picnics
- Outings

Home and social events: A great leader once said "No success can compensate for failure in the home." This is where the most communication – speaking – is needed and not much is done, at least not of the right kind. Family meetings, reunions, anniversaries, parties, all need something said well. Too often we think it's only when addressing the public – outsiders – that we need to call on our oratorial best. Not so! The first place is home.

Coaching and teaching situations: Every person at some time will be asked or involved in coaching or teaching. This is a chance not only to serve and help your family and community, but a key opportunity to touch and change the quality of individual lives. Effective speaking is the prime cog in the wheel of teaching others.

Church: Tired of dry sermons and professional preachers wailing at you? Who is more in touch with reality – with life, feelings, family, heartaches, pain, problems, and worries than the person who is right out in the midst of life – you? Churches are dying off from lack of fresh, interesting, inspiring speakers. And you can do as well or better than anyone you've heard from the pulpit. You have access to all of the religious and scriptural sources and material that anyone else does. And you have exactly the same right and credentials to present "religious" topics as any other. Funerals, weddings, receptions, always need able people to speak.

As soon as you learn to speak up, you'll have opportunities in all of these areas, and you'll do them easily and well.

Can I actually enjoy public speaking?

Speaking is more exciting than participating in or looking forward to a concert or athletic event, more emotional than a long-overdue meeting of two lovers, more stimulating than winning the lottery and even more rewarding in the long run – it's communication at its most exciting.

Once you learn how, where won't matter much. Like learning to hike or bicycle or jog, the terrain, country, weather, time of day, or equipment won't make much difference – once you know how, you can do it and enjoy it. But best of all you'll influence and affect lives and be rewarded with the greatest of all rewards. You will be loved for your service and accomplishments.

17

Chapter Two

Before you say a word

Be prepared. If you had to choose the most important message in this book, this would surely be it, because most of what makes a good speech is done before you ever stand up in front of an audience and open your mouth. I promise that if you're prepared, 95% of the fear of speaking will leave you. (You need the other 5% to keep you humble.) Preparation isn't a chore – it's easy, enjoyable, educational and the better you do it the harder it'll be to hold you back when your turn comes. There's a scripture that says: "If ye are prepared, ye have no fear." That's exactly the case with any speech you ever give. But you have to do it yourself – you can't delegate to others what you feel and what you're looking for.

Coming up with a topic and sticking to it

If "they" are doing the asking and the paying, and you are a professional speaker or represent a profession, group or position then you'd better take the subject they give you, unless it's a total loser. I generally stick to or close to the subject that's given me, so that my hosts feel they are getting their money's worth. I do, of course, alter, adapt and bend things a little to fit my own talents and strong points.

Any adjusting of your subject should be made when you commit yourself to giving a speech. Generally, people won't mind it then. But the closer it gets to zero hour, the more reluctant anyone will be to change anything, and the harder any changes are on the preparation process – and your nerves.

You, of course, will do better with a subject you're familiar with and have a passion for. But even if methodically researching facts you aren't in love with poses a challenge, you can still do it. And you can weave a measure of your personality into even an alien topic. The American humorist, Will Rogers, could make any subject interesting, funny and educational because he "Will Rogered it." You can do the same – you can personalize your material (when I do this I call it "Aslettizing").

TONIGHT
EVERYTHING YOU
EVER WANTED TO
KNOW ABOUT
ANYTHING AND
MORE BESIDES

Does the title of your talk matter?

Having to give your talk a name or a title can be a real disadvantage because it cuts out the flexibility of a last-minute change in emphasis. But of course everyone wants to know "What are you going to talk about?" They need a title to use in brochures, posters and pre-publicity. And people are going to read the title and decide right then and there whether they

like it or not, and whether they'll come or not.

You want your title to be catchy but appropriate – if your talk is going to be humorous, then a funny title is fine, but don't try to lure people to a serious talk with a wacky sounding title. I play a little sly and go for generic titles that can mean just about anything and cover all areas and give me back some of that subject flexibility. No one can fully understand them so they can't pin me down and they usually won't question me further. Here are some examples of this type of title which I have used in talking about cleaning, since that is my line of work: "The Bad Logic of Being Average," "From Outhouse to Penthouse," "Being Number One in a Number Two Business," "A Toilet Cleaner's Attitude," "Cleanliness Is Next to Godliness."

Believe me, if you give a good speech, well-suited to the occasion and to the audience, no one will worry about whether it precisely matched the title they first read or heard announced.

When should you start preparing your speech?

About four seconds after you've been asked to present it – even if your speaking date is nine months from now. Trust me, your best ideas, the fastest pace and the most progress will be made on your speech right when you are asked to do it – that's when your enthusiasm is at its peak. Here's

19

what works for me, and it can work for you too:

Someone asks you to speak to their group in May of the coming year, and you agree. Then ask:

★ "What am I speaking on and to whom?" – when they answer, write it down.

★ "What does your group want, need or like?" – write it down.

★ "Is there any subject or topic you would suggest?" – write it down.

★ "Who spoke last year and how did it go?" – write it down.

After you've hung up the telephone, jot down all your first thoughts on the subject. Then start a file on your speech. For the next month or year or whatever, when you run across a good idea, story, saying, or visual to do with your subject, put it in your file. It's amazing how soon you'll have more than enough information to choose from – then it's just a matter of organizing it.

Organizing your speech

The first thing you do after starting your file is make an initial outline. Look over all your first thoughts on the subject. Then write or type up a rough outline of the richest ore, the real bedrock ideas. Put the ideas in order, so that one leads logically to the next. Write down the connecting thoughts as soon as you have them. You are plotting the flight path of your speech and the connections are as important as whatever concepts you will be talking about. This doesn't mean you have to write it all out in elaborate complete sentences – just be sure to capture and record the basic thoughts and the angle you want to come at them from.

Carry the file and rough outline with you wherever you go for a week or two. It'll work like flypaper – ideas will fly in and stick to it. Once you have the structure of the outline and a little time, I promise that ideas, opportunities and help will flow into your mind without a lot of actual "sitting at the desk" time.

Most of my major addresses haven't had ten straight minutes of time on them, but maybe a month of spare minutes and casual consideration. If I need hard facts, statistics, research or visuals, a phone call or letter to the right place a couple of months ahead brings all the assistance I need (mostly free). If you're a beginner, you'll obviously need to spend more time and effort on your speech, but I promise you that if you use my speech preparation techniques, you'll soon be able to assemble an excellent presentation quickly and easily.

Know your audience before you prepare a speech for them

My college speech teacher Clark Carlile's best advice ever to me was: *PRE-ASSESS – THINK OF YOUR AUDIENCE.* While I'm gathering my material I think about the age and background of the audience, the season, the facility, the date, time of day, who else is going to speak and so on. I want to adapt my material to the particular audience and event. This means finding out what kind of people are likely to come. How old are they? What are their occupations? What is their social standing? Their level of education? Their religion? Their prejudices and beliefs? Are they wealthy, or of modest means? What, if anything, do they already know about

the subject? What do they want from me?

Over the years I have worked up a formal questionnaire (see page 22) to help me with my preparation (it's OK to copy and use this yourself). On the first call I have the framework I need and I gradually put it to use. This isn't only a good record and backup to have on hand, it also forces me to think of all the preparation areas, like making sure I have directions, that I might otherwise forget or neglect.

On my speaking confirmation form I ask if there are any skeletons in the closet, any political conflicts going on, power struggles, a recent death, or serious illness – this is a big help. Someone will tell me, "This town is generally offended by fast-talking Yankees," so I've been warned. Then I either talk slower or find a winning way to "excuse" myself for being a Yankee near the beginning of my speech. The little notes and warnings I get here prevent me ever standing up to give a standard Sunday school talk to a crowd on the verge of a riot.

Don Aslett Speaking Confirmation

Please Retain This Copy For Your File

Name of Vendor/Group requesting Don Aslett: _____

Contact Person: _____

Phone _____Office _____ Home

Presentation Scheduled for _____ / _____ / _____
　　　　　　　　　　　　　　　　Month　　　　Day　　　Year

Building _____

Address _____

Room _____

Theme/Subject of presentation: _____

Time Allotted:　From: _____　to _____

Approximately: _____hr. _____ minutes

Time room/place will be available for Don's set up:_____

Flight: _____

Arrival Time: _____

Hotel: _____　Phone: _____

Address: _____

Confirmed: _____□ from your group _____ □ from our office

Visual/Audio Needs:

Compensation: _____

Expenses: _____

_____ Expenses □　Shared □

Brochure/Literature Sent □　　Are Maps/Directions In File? □

　　　　　　　　Posters Sent □

IMPORTANT: Any political, social or physical problems brewing in the company or area, skeletons in the closet, or troublesome personalities I should be aware of, PLEASE NOTE HERE

_____
Don Aslett

_____
Vendor

If any of the above information is incorrect or needs to be changed, please notify our office immediately.

When is a scrubber not a cleaner? Watch those regional variations.

When you're in other countries (or other parts of your own country) that speak the "same" language, it may pay to do a little research or ask your hosts for a little primer of key words/regional slang that may be different within your subject matter. For example, when is a scrubber not a cleaner? When in England! On my first publicity tour of Great Britain, I experienced a few red-faced situations. All because of the little differences between the "English" spoken in the UK, and in the US. I did know that the word "janitor" wasn't readily recognized in Great Britain.

So on a national BBC interview with ten million listeners, when the host asked me what I did for a living in the US, I coolly answered "Oh, I'm just a scrubber from Idaho."

Everyone in the studio gasped and the interviewer covered the microphone. After the broadcast they informed me that a scrubber in Great Britain is a "hooker," or prostitute.

The next day I managed to do it again. I told the audience about a new handy tool to clean floors – cheap and effective and easy to use. Then I boldly said "What all you people in England need is a Doodlebug."

Again, everyone drew their breath in horror. At the conclusion of the show it was explained to me that a Doodlebug is the name of the whistling bomb that the Germans pelted England with during the war. Everyone in Great Britain had learned to turn in terror at the name "Doodlebug."

Watching those "little words" that slip out (bugger, crap, etc.) is a good idea too.

Appraise your speaking position

And fit it. If you are the main show, you have lots of flexibility. However, if you are an appendage, a supplement to the main event, then don't steal everyone else's show or time. As you prepare your speech keep in mind what the rest of the evening or afternoon is going to be like. Make sure your speech will be appropriate to the occasion, and to your relative importance in it.

The paring down process

As you approach the date of your talk you want to pare down the file and make a final outline. First you sort through the file, keeping only the ideas that really suit you, the subject, and the audience.

If, for example, you're speaking to a group of farmers on the importance of branding, you may have found treatises on the history of branding, fifty different methods and systems of branding, discussions and illustrations of a great variety of brand types, a full discussion on the legalitities surrounding the practice of branding, a description of how a branding iron is made, how branding irons are used as part of "rustic decor" today, and the like in reference books relating to branding.

Beware – don't go off on a tangent. Stick to the primary purpose of your address. The importance of identifying the cow and the simplest and safest and best way to do it. Sift through the fifty alternatives, many may be outdated, some too slow, cause infection etc., and select a few – the newest, the best, the pick of the herd – to present to your audience. The farmers will love it and learn it!

You give, not write, a speech

Once you have decided on your topic and title, pre-assessed your audience, sorted through your file and made a rough outline, you write out your speech, right? Wrong!

You don't write a speech, you write books and brochures and letters and give them to people to read. When you speak you are the message, and you can't be written. Staged, outlined and directed, maybe, but not written. You give speeches, you don't write them. Nor do you ask anyone else to write them.

Writing can never be as free and as in touch with the subtle and ever-changing human interplays of a live event. It's like love, you can try to write words about your feelings, but nothing communicates like action and speaking is action – not just verbalizing written words. It's vitally important for you to embrace this concept if you're going to speak vividly instead of in black and white!

Whenever you get up there and wrinkle your brow and roll your eyes, trying to "read" your talk, you begin to lose most of the audience. As well as all the fun of communicating.

The only actual writing on a speech is done in a very short form – when you make your final outline (see page 34) to organize your material and to jog your memory so you won't leave something out.

But maybe a professional should write it for you?

There might be some occasional

...to introduce myself – full stop – new paragraph – However – comma...

24

special need for a professional speechwriter, but in general I feel that asking someone to write a speech for you is as hopeless as asking someone to eat, play, exercise, or have sex for you.

Professional speech writing is sad evidence that you really don't have anything to say. When you have to hire someone to write your message, it automatically isn't your message. Even if you give the speechwriter your ideas, it's not the information the audience wants, it's your presentation of it – that's why they didn't ask the speechwriter to do it in the first place. If all that was needed was the facts, they could just pass around a book or fact sheet. Position, power, or schedule don't excuse anyone from preparing his or her own message. A message can't be very important if it isn't important enough for you to prepare personally.

Don't try to write it down and then memorize it, either

These are exactly the practices that give speaking its reputation as a bore and an ordeal! Imagine how restrictive it would be if before a visit, a date, a sales call, you wrote out everything you were going to present, memorized it, and then delivered it perfectly. It's ridiculous to even think about it.

You can speak to one hundred or one thousand as easily and effectively as you spontaneously converse at dinner, or at work.

Now, don't you memorizers panic and say "but the outcome might be totally unpredictable if I don't get it just right." The solution is the simple, sparsely-worded outline you have been preparing to be completely sure that you won't forget something, and that you will be able to keep it all in sequence and order. If you know your material and what you basically want to say, you need only key words and phrases to trigger the subject in your mind. People love spontaneity.

Besides, no matter how good your memory or your mind is, it'll trick you when you get into a pressured situation. In my youth, I learned this lesson, the best lesson of my speaking career, the hard way. I wrote out a brilliant speech, and memorized it to the letter, rehearsing arm gestures, voice gruffing, lip curling and all the accompaniments. I lived and relived that delivery six hundred times during the two weeks prior to the event. But when the big day came, I vaulted up the stairs to the stage and announced my subject, then looked out at the seven hundred students in the audience and my mind went blank. I mean blank, blank, blank. I couldn't find one word of that whole two minutes I'd memorized. My memory had failed, with disastrous results. I stood there silent for the whole two minutes.

Millions of people have had similar experiences and have quit speaking, thinking they weren't cut out for it. Like me when I was sixteen they didn't realize that **Memorization has nothing to do with speaking.**

The young minister was giving his first after-dinner speech in front of a large audience, and he felt extremely nervous. Before long, he gave up. "My dear friends," he told his listeners, "when I came here this evening only God and I knew what I planned to say to you – now only God knows!"

Rules and refresher

★ *Be prepared – and that means starting work on your speech the moment you agree to it.*

★ *Be informed – find out as much as you can about the audience, the event, the facility, etc.*

Chapter Three

You don't just give a speech, you present it

Now that you know you're going to make an outline, what are you going to outline? More than just your subject and materials. You need to outline an approach as well, a *presentation*. You want your outline to contain not just the points you want to make but *how* you intend to make them.

Seduction would be about the right word to describe how you present your subject in a good speech. The bottom line is that if you're going to succeed, you don't just blunder in and start up. Watch a skilled person, watch a good lawyer, watch a sales assistant, watch any real professional approach their job. They don't just walk up and start working away, shout out an accusation, come out and say "Will you buy this?" They all spend lots of time carefully choosing and preparing their approach and it makes all the difference. Once you've collected your material you want to sit down and think out how best to present it; what techniques to use – and which to avoid – in order to win over the audience.

Preparing a seduction

Think about your message, think about the point you're really trying to make. Then think about a way to dramatize that point. Let's say you've been selected by all two hundred parents to represent them at the next school board meeting and express their dissatisfaction with the new hot lunches – namely, the quality of the food the new food service is giving your children.

27

You accept of course, gather all the facts, consider all the opinions and questions, make a list of the complaints and you are basically ready to go in there and give them the word. But no – you might be prepared to give an accurate, understandable message, but they might not be moved to do anything at all about it. It's all in your presentation. Are you going to be tough, funny, argumentative, begging, threatening, all of the above? The board is going to be ready and waiting for you with an equal number of facts; they're sharp, they're old pros at this and used to people like you coming in and moaning and whining away. If ten of us had one hour to think up a brilliant approach to this talk, we would all come up with something good, much more effective than the usual stand up and state your business, while heads nod in a smoke-filled room. What would you do? Here's what I would do:

I'd send some spies out a few days in advance and find out exactly what the children have for lunch, and actually smuggle some of the most awful stuff out. Then when I went to the meeting ("Who's next? OK, Mr. Aslett.") before I said a word, I'd ask three or four of the two hundred people I was representing to come forward and set a tray of this food in front of each board member. Then I'd start: "The subject I want to address tonight is in front of each of you. You may eat as I talk, if you wish."

Then I'd immediately defuse the whole room and the board members by thanking and praising them for any other improvements they've made in the school recently – and explain that though the new bulletin boards, desks and curtains all serve the students' need for information and inspiration, health still comes first and what we eat is largely what makes for good health. I'd then show the absence record of the school, pointing out that the school loses money every time a student is absent. (I'd insinuate that malnutrition had a lot to do with all those 'flu and cold absences.) Now that I had their attention, I'd ask them: "How is the food? Would you care to eat this every day of the academic year?"

If you've got a message, use it!

If a person stands up to speak to the city council and says, "We need a stoplight at the intersection of 3rd Street and Whitman Avenue. It'll cost $350 and can save lives," then rattles off a list of dry statistics, he hasn't put across his message and won't gain the audience's support. A skilled speaker would do it this way, "Last Friday, at 3rd and Whitman, little John Doe's life was ended at the age of 4 years ... two months ago, at this same intersection the Reverend and Sister Smith were struck by a van. It was an accident, but explain that to the Widow Smith now. In the past three years, seventeen accidents of various degrees of seriousness have happened at that intersection, totalling a quarter of a million in insurance and damage, not to mention the immeasurable cost in human misery. Is 3rd and Whitman worth a $350 traffic light?" This speaker will get the light because he's made his message felt, he's described it as well as stated it. Always do this at the beginning – let them know *why* you are speaking about *what*.

How many quotations should you use?

Most new speakers, feeling their inadequacies, try to shore up the show by quoting the great and even the not-so-great: "and as ...... said it so well ..." Most speeches don't need this, besides, if it's worth quoting, tell the audience you agree with so-and-so when he said _____ (and sum it up in a sentence or two of your own). Think of how hard quotes can be to understand when you read them the first time – well, hearing is even trickier. If you must quote, keep your quotes short, like "War is hell," or "I shall return." I know there are thousands of books full of quotes by Emerson, Socrates, Shakespeare, George Washington, and Hagär the Horrible, just aching to be shot out to your audience, but it really doesn't do that much for you and a lot less for your talk!

I beg you to rely first on your own ingenuity. People want to hear from and about you – you have as interesting a life and record and as important a message – and opinion – as anyone in the world. So search your own mental and emotional library and storehouse for good material. Then you can refine and touch up your talk, if you like, with quotes or ideas from a few famous sources. But remember, the more personal a speech, the better people like it. Even if you do quote someone else, try to pick a person that you know or have had at least some interaction with.

For example: "As Jane Fonda said to me when I had a chance to meet her in a studio green room ..." is better than "Jane Fonda once said ..." And "my father-in-law always says ..." is better than "As Winston Churchill said ..."

Justifying your subject

A simple explanation is a great tool of communication, in ordinary conversation or public speaking. Everyone subconsciously has to have a reason to be sitting there watching your mouth move and words come out. They don't and won't wait until the middle of your speech to find out if the message is important to them or not. They rightfully want to know your reason for using their time (and it better be good!). Justifying a subject is nothing more than convincing the audience of its importance. Let me give you three examples of this:

1. You're giving a presentation on "How to Pack Your Own Parachute"
   Standard opening: "Today we're going to learn how to pack our own chutes. I'll give you the 1-2-3-4 instructions and then all of you can pack your own chutes."

   Justifying the subject: "When you jump out of the plane next week your chute will do one of two things – open or not open. If it opens, that means you probably listened to me today. If it doesn't open you won't have to repeat this class, and that's a promise. Now for the instructions...."

2. You're giving a presentation on the assigned subject of "Respecting the Flag"
   Standard opening: "True and loyal citizens respect their flag because it represents a great heritage of a great nation."

   Justifying the subject: "How many of you have ever been on a trip to a foreign country? How many of you gained from that trip a deeper appreciation for the place you live? How many of you would like to keep the freedoms you have now? It's up to all of us to make sure we keep them, and our reminder of this is our flag. Its job is not just waving...."

3. You're giving a speech on how to find work.
   Standard opening: Government statistics show that 8% of our citizens at any given point are unemployed and looking for work. Just where and how do you look for work?"

   Justifying the subject: You've been fired. Everyone in here is fired as of right now, you have no job. You are unemployed! Some of you are smiling comfortably and saying to yourself, "It can't happen to me." Did you know that last month 28,000 people, secure in their jobs and positions for sixteen years or more, were told to go with not much more than "thanks" and a good record?

Starters that need to stop!

Those first words that come out of your mouth can immediately close minds or open hearts. Put some time and thought into your opening line – and avoid at all costs the following:

★ **The definition:** "I looked (your subject matter) up in the dictionary and that is what it said" – this is a poor and incredibly overworked approach. No one needs a definition read to them, tell them what something means in your own words if you need to.

★ **Phrases people have had their fill of:** "I'd like to tell you a story ..." "OK, if you'll give me your attention ..." "Today we're going to talk about ..." "I'd like to tell you ..." "Our lesson today is ..." "I remember when ..."

★ **A piece of poetry.** Poetry reading is sure death in most speeches or presentations. No matter how eloquent or perfectly suitable the statement, your chances of getting your audience to appreciate it are nil. Once in a while a short springy little verse will succeed, but most of the time you'll flop. Most poetry readers further poison their plot by announcing "Now, I'd like to read you a little poem." That's a turn-off. If you have a hopeless addiction to Wordsworth, run home and look up your most treasured poems and read and enjoy them and think about them, but spare the audience.

> *Just remember that you're allowed to be opinionated, but not judgmental.*
> ★ *Speeding is no good and anyone caught ought to be thrown in jail ... (judgmental)*
> ★ *If I were speeding, I'd expect them to jail me if they caught me ... (opinion)*
> ★ *You should ... is preachy and judgmental*
> ★ *We should ... is opinionated and persuasive*

Personalize, don't plagiarize

People want to hear you, not your condensation and summary of forty other predecessors. People hate the "Ladies and gentlemen, we must be prepared to meet the coming challenge" talk and the typical mayoral/graduation/political speeches turn people off. They want to know how *you* propose that they meet and solve present or coming problems. They don't need someone else's analysis and appraisal, they want to know what

First I'd like to read you a little po...

to do, how, when and why from **you**. Even if you're wrong, they'd rather have the benefit of your judgment. They want personal help, direction, assurance, not a list of someone else's facts. Even if your opinion or appraisal is different from anyone else's, it's your opinion and there is value in it.

Don't bother using big words

As a new speaker you'll often feel pretty small in ability compared to all the big talkers you've seen or read about. So you may think that if you use a few big words like you imagine the biggies do, it'll let the audience know you're in full command of the language, and boost your image. The fact is that most of the audience won't understand any word you had to look up, so just be yourself. When you use a word or words you're unfamiliar and uncomfortable with, it'll really stand out and

show. I'd rather see someone use a word they made up than one they had to look up.

What about using jokes?

People love to laugh. They want to laugh even in serious business presentations and in dry financial reporting, in the classroom, seminar, and yes, there's even a time for it at funerals. When people laugh, they relax and they remember you and your message better. And audiences will stimulate each other to even greater heights of laughter, once you get them started.

Of course, being funny is easier said than done. And all of us can think of people we know who try to tell jokes and can't. Nothing is worse than trying to be funny and not quite accomplishing it. Learning to present a humorous speech is like developing muscles, you get a few aches and pains from the first few tries, but every day and every speech you get better. Use three or four humorous stories that you've had in mind, or have heard and liked. Watch how your audience reacts, and dump the poor or mediocre ones and keep the good. After about ten talks you should have a little battery of funny stories that you love to tell and you know will work.

Stay away from the joke books

Keep your jokes and funny stories honest, truthful, real, everyday.

32

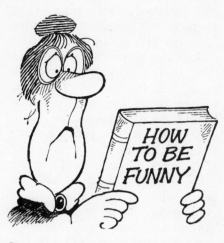

Stay away from the "how to be funny" 1001 funny anecdote and joke books and canned lines. Those are for the hopelessly dry professionals and the would-be funny men. Stick to your own idea of what's funny – grab what you hear and see around you and in your own life, fit it into the subject matter, and tell it well. People will love it because it's real and it's yours. On stage, for example, I often demonstrate how most people vacuum. I repeat all the struggles with the vacuum we've all experienced. My audiences go into tears of laughter for fifteen minutes and roar until I finish. All I'm doing is exactly what every one of *them* has done, with a little more noise and exaggeration.

Poke fun at yourself, not other people

Making fun of yourself is always a safe bet, telling the most embarrassing things that happened to you relating to the subject at hand,

for example, usually goes over well. But keep the jokes close to home – them, us, you, me – not the other guys.

- You never – to any group – want to use ethnic jokes, and stay away from making fun of specific individuals, too. It's tempting, but tricky. If you want to tell a joke pick on a group like accountants or lawyers – we don't mind our professions being chided a little and the attention is usually appreciated, but stay away from race, religion, creed, and ethnic origin.
- Never start your funny story or joke with: "I have a funny story …" or "I heard this joke …"
- Keep your jokes and stories clean. Never, never use crude, risqué, or profane material. No audience is adult enough for this. Most people are offended by jokes in poor taste – don't risk it. Leave out the dirty jokes – I assure you, for every one that goes across, five will return to haunt you.

How should a speech end?

Your ending should be sharp as a cliff, not a winding down, a gradual slope into nothing. I disagree with all the speech experts who say before you end, give a summary of what you said. People should and will understand you the first time, if you're doing your job. In my opinion a summary at the end, when you and the audience are getting weary, only detracts from and dilutes the drama of a well done presentation – it's like digging up a grave after a funeral to see if everything's OK.

Unless you have a performance other than the words you speak (a display, a short dance, a demonstration, etc.) when you're finished with your message your speech is long enough.

So at the end of a talk plan to simply and briefly reaffirm your basic stand, your basic advice on the topic and let the audience know you expect great things out of them. Put the responsibility of the message on their shoulders as you end. Leave them with "Well now you know and believe, what are you going to do about it?" "I'm confident that you're all going to go out and start to lose those extra ten pounds this very week." Then I always hold up my hand and wave a thank you.

Making your final outline

An outline is what you will take

They won't go to sleep — can I borrow your speech for a minute?

with you to the stage or speaking platform. It contains the order of your presentation, plus the specifics of any facts or statistics you don't want to have to memorize. It tells you when you will be using any visual aids. It should also have noted on it a halfway point so that you can keep track of the time.

A speech is made up of a beginning, a middle, and an end. Or an opening, a main body, and a conclusion. Your initial, rough outline has your basic sequence and your best ideas. You'll be surprised just how much of it you'll still find useful. You've gone through and pared down your material to suit this speech and this audience. You've thought about your approach and your presentation. You know what your main message is. And you've thought out your opening.

So start the outline by noting your opening line down at the top of a sheet of paper. Then, referring to your rough outline and remembering you don't want to go off on tangents, put down the rest of your speech as a series of headings. If there's something particular you want to be sure to say, list it under the appropriate heading. If you're going to use a quotation, write it down under the heading where you intend to use it. Estimate that each heading represents about ten or fifteen minutes talking time. Your conclusion should be a short, *very* short, summary of what you've said – in other words, restate your message in a single sentence if at all possible. Write that entire sentence down so you won't forget – a memorable, smart conclusion is just as important as a dramatic opening.

Try to edit your outline down to a single sheet of paper. You want to avoid rustling and rattling noises crackling into the microphone and interfering with your presentation. As long as it's a map that you can refer to quickly and easily your outline will work. Just remember that an outline is basically a way for you, the speaker, to keep track of the content and the order of your talk, so it can be very short and concise and skeleton like or in your own brand of shorthand (see my outline, page 37). No one else has to understand it – just as long as you can follow what you've written. The briefer the better, because you can refer to it and tell where you go next much more quickly and easily.

Your outline will give you the security that your speech is well-planned without robbing you of your natural delivery. You can relax and use the words that come naturally to mind to express each thought in the thought chain. I've given more than eight thousand speeches of all kinds, to all kinds of audiences, in all kinds of places, and all I ever use is an outline, **and my own words**.

Rehearsing the speech

The popular concept of rehearsing a talk shows one spouse trying out a speech on the other or in front

of a mirror. Don't worry about the experience in front of an audience – believe it or not, your best "rehearsal" will come as you develop your outline and put together your visual aids (see chapter eight, page 81). As you do this you construct and reinforce the main artery of your speech from which you will branch off on small, *short* veins of thought. As you do this you are mentally giving small pieces of your talk.

If you are making a speech for the first time, you can rehearse giving the speech from your outline a few times – this will help

you time the speech and cut out any unnecessary fat. You can also give the speech to an empty room with a tape recorder in it and then play back the tape. This will help you get used to the sound of your own voice and make you aware of any unconscious verbal mannerisms, like starting every sentence with "I" or ending every other sentence with "ummm."

If, as you talk, you come up with some great lines, so much the better. Jot them down on your outline so that you can use them when it's time for the real thing.

A few rehearsals will give you all the confidence you'll need in your outline and your ability to speak from it – and help you make that outline as polished and to the point as possible.

Clark Carlile, my college speech teacher, always taught his students to outline in complete sentences. After several thousand speeches, I gradually began to modify that to a shorter, "code" version with just a series of key words in the right sequence. Once you really get to know the material of a speech, this is like walking familiar territory with a general map instead of a detail map. Opposite is an example of one of my outlines, just to give you an idea of what an outline might look like. I am trying to convince wives of Boy Scouts of America executives to contribute more time and effort to scouting.

Eventually, as a veteran speaker, your outline will evolve into a similar "code page," needing only half a glance to lead you elegantly through your speech.

Joys of Leadership
For Wives of B.S.A. Executives

I. **My Scouting/Cleaning Career**
  a. Toilet Light Demo
  b. Canteen Cleaning

II. **Doing Well in Life**
  a. 65% Career Planned
  b. Only 15% Life Planned
  c. Failure or Success? (Both benefit)

III. **Illusions**
  a. Others Making More (Sacrifice)
  b. Having Is Everything (Loving is Everything)
  c. Get Off the Firing Line (Changing Lives)

IV. **My Leadership History Book (Scout Book)**
  a. Why Not You?
  b. Who Better?
  c. No Time?
  d. No Talent?

V. **Decision & Commitment**
  a. Indecisive Pig Demo
  b. 3-Phase Plan
  c. Gorilla Story

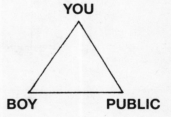

VI. **Volunteering, Service, Sacrifice**
  a. Jamboree = Two Sons-in-law

VII. **Image-size of People Not Related to Size of Town**

Timing your speech

Timing is easy with an outline. With an outline you can judge about where the halfway point in your speech should be and where and when you should begin your wrap-up. You can't expect timing to always be exact, though, because the exact same speech that took forty-five minutes in front of the mirror, in front of an audience may include laughter, comments and exchanges with the audience, a late start, etc. that can double your actual speaking time – it's happened to me many times! Still, you should run through your outline and mark an approximate halfway point as well as a "You have five minutes left" point. If you know when you're going to start speaking you can write on the outline the time you should be halfway through: "8:45." Then you can glance at the clock and glance at the outline and know just how you're doing for time. When you make your estimate, be generous – it will take longer live!

Rules and refresher

★ *Be yourself* – *steer clear of quotations, big words, other people's ideas. Use your own words and your own jokes to express your own point of view.*

★ *Be clever* – *consider your approach, your message, how you're going to sell your speech – that means really working on your opening.*

Chapter Four

The right frame of mind

For a week before a big game in school or college, we athletes would prepare. No dates, sweets, etc. to distract our emotions or physical strength. Then on the big day itself our coach would always prepare us with a light practice session, a little relaxing, then a little stirring of the adrenaline, looking at our opponents' pictures and records. By the time the starting whistle blew, we were full of spirit and energy.

Speaking engagements are more demanding than any game I've ever played in. An hour of speaking drains more energy out of you than an hour of hard running on the field. Yet few speakers or performers prepare for it and often approach the platform with their edge gone, worn off by pre-speaking activities and distractions. In order to present your speech well, you need to be in top form, relaxed and full of confidence. That means doing a little research ahead of time – and avoiding last minute hassles and problems. The frame of mind you're in as you stand up to speak is as important as the speech itself.

Don't eat, drink and be merry

Several hours of hard driving, long intense interviews, loud dinners, listening to once-in-a-lifetime business opportunities right before I speak zaps most of my spark and inspiration. If you have a speech to give, do your socializing later. I seldom eat before speaking, even if I'm seated at the head table. A little hunger makes your body and train of thought function better. I hate to sit at the head table and eat stale rolls and rubbery peas and then have to stand up with stringy cold meat still lodged between my

teeth. There's no way to eat gracefully in front of people. If you're the focus of attention, avoid it. If you can't, eat something light. Don't drink or otherwise wear yourself out, or try to artificially fortify yourself, for that matter. Go on stage with a clear head and clean countenance.

What's the schedule?

Ask the host to send you the folder or kit on the event as soon as possible, so you know where your speech falls, and what activities, breaks, etc. occur before, during and after you. (It'll prevent you from wearing a suit when your talk is around a campfire.)

Get directions!

Driving up and down roads hunting hysterically for "the place" in rush hour traffic can be avoided with some forward planning.

No matter how well you know the town, or who is going to pick you up, or how much time you

ASSEMBLY ROOMS

have to find the place where you're going to speak or perform, request a simple, complete map and full address and phone number if possible. Nothing will ruin the spirit of a speech as much as getting sweaty and upset trying to find the right building or the right room. "In the Sheraton Hotel" isn't enough – you want the room and floor and the street address and for that matter exactly which Sheraton it is. Often even the convention or reception or building manager doesn't know where you belong. It's especially important to know where you're going since you're going to be early and you won't necessarily have a crowd to guide you to the spot.

Know where you're going to stay, how you're going to get there

If at all possible stay in or near the site of your engagement. Nothing will more benefit your job of entertaining or teaching a group than living amid, associating with, hanging around with, and casually conversing with members of the group. It can really get you in the spirit of the occasion. Not only will you pick up on the "in" happenings and the inside jokes and become an insider, you'll eliminate the stress and tension of getting to and from the location. If you have props, staying "on location" will save all that suit-splitting, hose-snagging loading and unloading and no-parking area parking. I always experience a great sense of calm when I'm told, "By the way, you're staying in the hotel where you'll be speaking."

Otherwise find out from your host how they plan to get you from your hotel to the speaking venue. If you're arriving on the day of the speech, find out whether someone will collect you at the airport or train station – make sure you know exactly where you'll meet that person, how you'll recognize him or her. If you're making your own way, work out in advance exactly how you'll get to the engagement and how long it will take. Even if your host says someone will meet you, you might as well find out about getting there on your own, just in case.

Be on time – better still, be early

The frame of mind you're in when standing up to speak is as important as the speech itself. If you're unsure, late, or irritated, you'll do poorly.

Never plan arrival times and travel to the last minute – too much can go wrong. Traffic jams, bad weather, lost keys, lost luggage – all kinds of things can go wrong. An accident can cause you to be late or miss your appointment. Nothing may happen, but if a little catastrophe does crop up you have it covered by being early.

So be early, ridiculously early. Being early has almost as much bearing on your presentation as your delivery of it. No successful trek was ever made without scouting the area before settling in. When you beat everyone there you can:

- case the place
- rearrange seating
- locate your name tag and place card
- check the layout
- make sure there's room for all the activities you have in mind
- set up your props
- test the sound
- find a parking place
- locate the toilet (this is . crucial!)
- review the schedule

In short, you can be prepared and in confident control, physically and emotionally. You have time to make friends with and learn the names of the waiter, the convention leaders, the TV crew, the doorman, and the host, who will later break all records to help you do your best.

Sit in several different spots in the audience area and get a feel for the set up, then you'll be comfortable and assured and won't have to ask the audience "Can you see? Can you hear me ... is this all right?"

When I go to one of my presentations I'm often there before they unlock the building. At the very least, I get to the TV station or speaking place one hour before anybody else. It feels good and there's time to get everything ready and then clean myself up.

Remember that a professional doesn't have to ask how things are because he or she knows ahead of time. Being early gives you a real edge and that extra confidence that makes the difference.

Do some last minute tailoring on your talk

You want to go to your speech totally prepared, but then once you're there (early!), you can do the final tailoring of your talk to the people, facility, weather, and the spirit of the gathering, after you look at the people and get adjusted to the place. Always check out the other activities in the area. I once did a long pre-arranged live (three hours of solid entertainment) seminar in a small mountain town. I detected a subdued response and found out later that a couple of hours after me in the same auditorium, they were holding a double funeral for two little girls killed in an accident a few days earlier. Had I discovered it prior to my presentation, I could have been much more gracious.

Now I make it a practice to buy and read the local papers before a speech, including the advertisements. It's amazing how much you can pick up to sprinkle in your speech the next day and give a thoughtful little custom-made touch to your message. If the main factory in the city employing one-third of the town has just closed

down, the audience wants you to know and weep a little with them, then they'll listen.

What's the dress code?

There's enough to concern yourself with when you're making a presentation without being constantly concerned with your appearance or grooming. When you're on stage everyone sees you for a long time – they see you move, laugh, lift your arms and gesture. If you have distracting flaws, they'll be noticed by you first, and the audience next, and they can kill your speech as well as embarrass you. If anything in

your dress or physical appearance is going to bother you, be aware of it before your presentation and take care of it, don't try to bluff past it. (This means things like too long a tie, a gravy spot or a wet spot anywhere, backlighting illuminating everything through your dress, glasses slipping down your nose, false eyelashes falling.)

Most of your dress code worries will disappear when you do your audience pre-assessment long before you speak. Then if there's any doubt about it, simply ask the host if they have any feelings about what you should wear. Tell them what you plan to wear and they'll suggest any adjustments necessary and you'll be in business. **Dressing up is safer than dressing down**; even if the group is doing something wild after your presentation, you don't necessarily have to be a part of it. And if you do, you can be a little overdressed for the occasion, as "the speaker." I spoke to an American Express group in Phoenix, Arizona and right afer my speech they were scheduled to jump into buses and go out to a western-style ranch for Western entertainment and steaks around a campfire. Many of them came dressed for the West, but I wore a smart blue suit to fit my presentation. (I did join the round up later, but just used a bigger napkin.) A cowboy shirt and boots wouldn't have been right for me as the speaker.

Check yourself over before you start to be sure you're totally presentable, then you won't have to worry and you can put all your effort into your talk.

Minutes before going on, double-check for:

- crooked tie or scarf
- smeared make up or uncovered blemishes
- open zippers, exposed shirt tails
- pens or papers sticking out of pockets
- spaghetti stuck to your jacket sleeve
- food stuck in your teeth
- slips showing or torn pantyhose

Your dress and manner can be relaxed, but not too casual. Some veteran speakers try to be "cool" and end up leaning, slouching, sipping water endlessly, yawning and coughing everywhere. Get all the distractions over with before you face anyone. Cleaning your glasses or blowing your nose in public is not cool.

P.S. Do stay aware of your environment after you get going. During a business after-dinner speech, I noticed some strange smirks and smiles in the audience and finally one friend made hand swipes over his head to me. After the event adjourned, my friend told me a giant, brilliant dragonfly had encircled my head and then settled there, just like a small helicopter, much to the delight and distraction of the audience.

Beware what you wear!

When you speak, your most serious competition can be yourself. Don't let your appearance outdo you or it will!

- **Keep your clothes simple**. Keep the patterns and styles simple. Don't hang ornaments or badges all over your clothes when you speak. Any physical object – even a flower hanging on you – distracts from your face. I even take off my convention name tag. A giant diamond tie pin (even a medium-sized one) will hurt your delivery. Half of the audience will be wondering what it's worth, what size, etc., it is, the other half will be jealous of you for having it or wondering if it's a cubic zirconium.

- **Leave the cigarettes behind**. A big bulging pack of cigarettes in a tight shirt pocket is really distracting to your dress. If you smoke leave your cigarettes at your chair. People have a lot of built-in prejudices and the whole time you're talking they'll say to themselves: "He's probably going to light up any minute."

- **Don't wear stripes**. On shirts, ties and blouses they will "strobe" on the audience's eyes and on the TV cameras, causing a constant and highly distracting hypnotic effect. And avoid glowing whites, too, because they will indeed glow.

- **Be appropriate**. Your subject and audience and the environmental conditions really dictate the dress code. Don't wear a full-skirted, flimsy cotton dress to an outside event where a gust of wind will have you looking like Marilyn Monroe.

- **Stick to your own size**. "Appropriate dress" means appropriate not only to the occasion or to the audience, but to yourself. If you can't lean down or move around because your gown, girdle, or sports coat is too tight or strained, you'll lose the audience, too. They'll be more concerned about the giving way of the fabric than the message you're giving.

- **Watch your feet**. Footwear is important to consider, too. I'm a mover on the stage, I do some quick turns and some fast footwork and even leaps in my cleaning concerts. Wearing leather-soled shoes caused plenty of embarrassing near falls. The day I graduated to some sturdy rubber-soled shoes was the saving of my spine and the extra grip and comfort improved the quality of my performance. Wobbling on toothpick-thin high heels isn't conducive to a comfortable delivery, either – or an entrance on tricky stairs, etc. The audience will be more concerned with your survival on the runway than the message you bring.

Don't let your personal appearance – or even your personal appeal – distract your audience from what you're saying.

A last minute meditation

The last second before you plunge into the icy water at camp, snatch the piece of cake and run for it, tell Herman Hiccups he is fired, say yes to the opportunity to speak at the national convention ... is like accelerated living – in a few seconds your whole life of values, dreams, regrets, directions, commitments, flashes through your brain and you ask yourself "Why am I here? Why am I doing this anyway?" and most important of all "If I get through this and do it well, what will I have accomplished?" All of these things are working in me right before I go on stage or in front of an audience, so I just put my head down for a few minutes and mentally review the situation, especially my responsibility to the audience and what I might be able to do for them, how I might be able to help them or change their lives for the better. I really try to forget about myself and think of the cause, why I'm there, the people who are assembled and then the hoped-for reward of doing well – then I'm ready to go.

Rules and refresher

★ **Be early** – *so that you can be calm, cool and collected when it is time to speak.*

★ **Be appropriate** – *especially when it comes to clothes, but also when it comes to any recent events that may have affected the people you're speaking to.*

Chapter Five

Set up for success

Controlling the situation you speak in

A speech can be a total failure because of the environmental conditions. It's happened to me, you've seen it happen to others, and it will undoubtedly eventually happen to you. The audience doesn't know where to sit, they can't hear, they can't see, no one knows what's going on and they're talking and rummaging the whole time. Meanwhile some poor slob is trying to deliver a message. It happens even in the best concert halls, college auditoriums and most sophisticated of conference rooms. Poor facilities and lack of organization can kill the finest speaker and his message. Let's never let it happen to us again.

In my first year of speaking I took what people gave me. They'd point at a place in the room, say "there you go" and I'd make the best of it. But not any more! Now, I tell them, and insist, how things must be – you can and should do the same. Remember, you're the performer, so people (hosts) will listen to you and go out of their way to accommodate you when you tell them how you want the seating, sound, tables, etc. If you're going to speak, you want to control the physical environment.

Gather some intelligence

No army, sports team, political party, salesman, or even doctor, will start a job without diagnosing the situation and getting information beforehand. I've found the easiest way to do this is by a simple request sheet. When a call or request comes, I ask most or all of these questions and in five minutes I've avoided twenty pitfalls, ten expensive follow-up calls and nervewracking last-minute questions. Make yourself one of these forms, adapt it to suit you, keep a pad of forms at your office or home and, regardless of who takes the call, you'll get all the information you need beforehand.

47

Speaking Request

Date of Request _____ Time of Request: _____

Request From: _____Company ☐   Private ☐

Name: _____ Phone: _____

Address: _____ Phone: _____Home

Speaking Occasion: **Purpose:**

☐ Convention   ☐ Entertainment   ☐ Inspiration
☐ Church gathering   ☐ Fund Raising   ☐ Other
☐ Business gathering   ☐ Motivation
☐ Social gathering

Date Wanted: _____ Alternative: _____

Deadline for Acceptance: _____

Place Held: _____

Will Mr. Aslett be the Keynote Speaker: ☐ Yes   ☐ No

What is the Occasion/Theme/Objective of the Presentation: _____

_____

How much outside publicity will he receive: _____

Audience: How many at event: _____ How many in Don's session: _____

Is this a closed group: ☐ Yes   ☐ No

Will the audience be: Male ____ Female ____ Mixed (what %?) _____

How much time will Mr. Aslett have: _____

Who will introduce Mr. Aslett: _____

Who/What will precede Mr. Aslett: _____ Topic: _____

Who/What will follow Mr. Aslett: _____ Topic: _____

When will Mr. Aslett's presentation come: ☐ First ☐ Middle ☐ End

Will food be served: ☐ Yes   ☐ No

Can he offer his books for sale: ☐ Yes   ☐ No

Can he distribute brochures: ☐ Yes   ☐ No

Will someone be able to assist him in preparation and set-up: _____

What is the parking situation and the ease of accessibility for transporting props:

_____

Compensation:

   Distance to travel: _____

   Travel Expense: _____

   Lodging: _____

Do you have a set fee or expense account to offer or would you like us to quote you

a price: _____ Price quoted or discussed: $/£ _____

Notes:

Try to arrange a good speaking time

Speaking during a meal is a real disadvantage. Many speeches are connected with luncheons, banquets, teas, toasts, etc., but food in any speaking situation can give a good speech indigestion. I'm totally against any eating, drinking, or table serving and clearing while I'm performing. It's an insult for a speaker (or any performer) to stand up and perform against a background of chomping and slurping, belching

and crunching. My refusal to be part of it has worked. If someone asks me to speak, I ask them if food or drink will be served during my speech. If they say "yes," I say "no." Without exception, everyone who really wants me sets the whole food process apart from my speech. I forbid any picking up of dishes, pouring of coffee, any movement at all, *and hosts*

respect this.

You can be a good after-dinner speaker, but never a successful during-dinner speaker. It's you or the food.

- *The world's best after-dinner speech – "Waiter, I'll pay for everyone."*
- *The world's most-common after-dinner lie – "Your speech will be at 8:00p.m."*

Speaking right before or right after lunch or dinner is definitely a disadvantage, but sometimes hard to avoid, so it may have to be viewed as one of those little evils of life. People love to eat and will, and someone still has to do the talking. When I speak after a meal I always try to include a hands-on project or two – something that involves the audience in moving, handling things, and taxing their brains. Activity will always overcome drowsiness and will inject a little fear (of "performing") in them that will help keep them awake.

Alas, you don't usually get much choice of "when" you speak. Generally the organization has a schedule and you have to fit into it. If you do get the chance to request your speaking time, try for around 9:00a.m. or 10:30a.m., or about 7:00-9:00p.m. in the evening. If you can swing it, pick the best times to speak – you'll have that many fewer distractions to contend with.

Check out the sound system

We can put men on the moon, but nobody can hear in the back row of the auditorium! This is the cry of thousands of lecturers who watch the people in their audience lose interest, doze, or pack up and leave, because they couldn't hear

or were annoyed by echoes, crackles or buzzing in the sound system. Problems like these ruin half a million speeches a week. Well, make that 499,999 – from now on, it won't happen to you. I've seen genuine talent and geat ideas go to waste because the audience couldn't understand the speaker. Don't assume that because it's a plush hotel, modern university or the world's second-largest political rally, that the stage and sound system will be free of interference and distractions. I was the main speaker at a convention at a university in its famous symphony hall. The heads of all the education boards were there. I assumed that after forty years of performances that hall would be equipped with a sound system. What

they had was a fold-up mike that made me sound like Mickey Mouse.

● Always find out weeks in advance how good the sound system is. If they hesitate or say "It works sometimes," etc., bring your own. The sound system and microphone is the host's responsibility, so don't be afraid to ask about it. In fact tell them what you require. It's surprising the authority you carry as "the speaker". I always ask how many will attend; if there's less than fifty I never use a mike unless it's an outdoor gathering. Fifty people is usually a compact enough group to use my normal voice.

● Always use a mike if there's any question about your audience's ability to hear you. Remember the front rows may be able to hear, but the side or back rows may not. Always use a mike if there's even a shadow of doubt. Never let an audience strain to hear, especially when you have to turn your back to write, etc.

● Always check and double-check the sound before you go on (at least an hour before). Make sure you get to the venue early enough to get the mike set up and perfectly adjusted. Know where the volume switches are and **know** if the audience can hear you, don't ask.

Always find out where and how (or by whom) the volume can be adjusted, then if you have to change it in the middle of a speech, you'll appear intelligent to the audience (which is just as baffled or mystified by mikes as you once were). Also make sure you know how to adjust the height of a mike that is fixed to a stand. The speaker before you could be five inches taller or shorter – you want to be able to confidently move to the microphone, adjust it to the correct height – just under your chin and facing upwards – and start speaking.

Make sure you meet the person responsible for "the sound" (it's always someone special, other than the host or doorman) and know where to find him/her.

Have a stand-by ready

Don't underestimate the value of double-checking all preparations and facilities. If there's any doubt at all, be prepared with a stand-by sound source/alternative mike. Fifty times I've had to switch to a stand-by and if I hadn't been prepared, I'd have missed giving my talk to thousands of people. It's hard for me to recommend renting a system because in my experience an over-keen electronics nut finds it necessary to fumble with and adjust the components all the way through a speech – distracting the audience. Rental fees are also expensive. When I've found myself without a microphone provided and I've left mine at home, I run down to a local electronics shop and buy a cheap mike that sounds clear and works easily. Consider getting your own, even if you just speak occasionally.

Don't be mike-shy

At our first speech (and often even at the second and third) most of us have a case of nerves that leaves us hoping – praying, even – that we won't be heard. After you gain control and confidence you'll demand to be heard – loud and clear. The microphone is nothing but a small tool to boost your voice a little for those in the back row, to outdo that persistent air conditioner and the other on-site noises inherent to auditoriums, conference rooms, etc.

One thing to your advantage is that microphones are getting better and better at picking up only the sound that they're directed at and more forgiving than ever of breathing or other distracting noises, so you can concentrate on your speech and delivery rather than on the mike. The choices you have here are:

1. Fixed. This means it's either on a stand or mounted and it never moves (so it means you're "fixed" too, because it limits your movement).

2. Hand-held. Just like it sounds, means one you hold in your hand. This means it can move with you. But, if you forget to hold it up when you're talking, your speech will be full of holes (although the cat-calls may help you remember: "Hold the mike up, you idiot").

3. Mobile or "Lavaliere" (lav'e-lîr') A mike worn like a big pendant on a loop around the neck or clipped to your tie or blouse. These are by far the best choice because they're inconspicuous, and leave both hands free. They turn mediocre delivery into dynamite by giving you the ability to move away from the platform. It stays close to your body, helping eliminate the noise made when your clothes rustle, and doesn't feel like an albatross hanging from your neck. A cord connects the mike on your lapel or wherever to the amplifier, so you can roam freely – or at least as far as the length of your cord.

The cord from the microphone can be laced under your shirt or skirt and will hardly be noticeable. The length of the cord you'll need depends upon how far you move when moving around the stage. Always make sure there's enough cord. If the cord on the mike isn't long enough you can buy a microphone extension cable. At the end of the cord is a male plug which connects into the female socket of whatever sound system you have to use. A good investment, if you're going to give many speeches, is to buy your own Lavaliere mike and carry it with you. When purchasing your microphone also buy a couple of adapters so you can always match the sound system available.

4. Remotes. These microphones are connected to a small radio transmitter, the size of a pack of cigarettes, that you hide in your pocket or clip to your belt, with a short cord up to the mike. These are great – no long cord to trip over or worry about, so you can move freely and concentrate on your speech. The disadvantages are that the battery can lose power or go dead if you don't keep an eye on it; you can have interference from some types of electrical lighting, or hit a "dead spot" on stage (where the mike's radio reception is blocked). And you may occasionally intercept a C.B. or police radio transmission. Check a remote mike out carefully prior to your presentation and don't forget about the on-off switch. Leave it on when you go off stage and you'll broadcast your cloakroom activities to the whole audience. These problems can be overcome though, and remote mikes are getting more popular all the time.

More mike mentions

- *The more subtly you use a mike, the better. Holding a giant hand-held one or having one block out your face while you're talking isn't going to do anything for your speech.*
- *When you use a microphone your audience still wants to see your face. Don't adjust the microphone so it covers your face. Keeping it at chin or chest level is better.*
- *Watch polyester clothes around a mike – if they rub against it, they make static.*
- *A microphone amplifies all sounds. Be careful not to rattle your notes or papers, burp, sniff or cough into it, etc.*

Check for disruptive noises

Speaking is surely one of the times in life when competition for attention is unwelcome. Many people, companies, hotels, etc. are totally insensitive to this. You want to control and eliminate all noise. Common problems are:

- **Piped-in background music.** Mood music, even played very soft or in a hall nearby, is distracting. If at all possible prevent through-the-wall music from competing with your performance.
- **Unexpected extra events.** In Sioux Falls I did a grand fanfare appearance for the Empire Shopping Mall. Aware of all the problems of busy malls, I checked and double-checked and everything was OK. The Empire people were 100% efficient on the sound system, stage, and props – except right in the middle of the mall where I was staged the front of a store was being rebuilt and carpenters were erecting walls. So I

had to talk over twenty screaming saws and hammers pounding thirty pounds of nails. Check and double-check your facility; simply ask if there's anything else, any action or distraction likely to be going on while you're performing?

- **Dishes rattling in the kitchen or hallway.** Or ice being poured or clinked in containers on tables, ashtrays being emptied, coffee or tea cups being refilled – be aware of these sounds you're competing against at any gathering where a meal is served. Food-scraping table clearers are about the most obnoxious disrupters of a presentation. Most meeting rooms in schools or hotels, even churches, are fairly close, if not right next to, the kitchen so food can be conveniently delivered hot and fast. All there is to block the horrible sound of two thousand clinking pieces of silverware, dishes, pans and the cavernous noises of the oven opening and closing are two swing doors (also noisy) with a four-inch gap between them. Some of the tables are right next to these doors, and as soon as the building's food staff have cleared the tables they have a shouting and dishwashing free-for-all. Sure their job is necessary, but unnecessary inconsiderate noise isn't. Service people clearing tables, replenishing tables, moving furniture, etc. can in most cases be prevented from doing so while you're speaking if you make a point about it beforehand with the sponsor, caterer, or maitre

54

d'hotel. Firmly state your requirements and insist that food service people refrain from entering the room while you speak.

Quiet, please!

As you notice on my speaking form, I request quiet right from the start, then ask again on arrival, and again just prior to speaking (to the host and head waiter). Then if they haven't taken me seriously, I request it during my presentation and embarrass them.

- **Banging doors.** Every speaking or performance place has one. Count on it and either fix it or comment on it briefly in your speech so people will ignore it from then on. Or come right out and ask, "Could someone please wedge that door open!"
- **Tape recorders.** "Can I record this, Mr. Aslett?" "Yes," I say, "but don't make any noise." That's like saying "eat popcorn and raw carrots quietly." People leaping up and down to service a clicking, snapping, squeaking recorder is a tremendous distraction

and probably outweighs the ego-flattery of believing someone wants to hear you twice. If you do say "yes," keep tapes quiet and out of the way and out of view of the audience. And, if at all possible, ask the person taping if they'll run you a cassette copy. It will be interesting and revealing to hear yourself give a talk.

Check the lighting situation

Getting plenty of light on you and the speaking area is a critical point. If you are the prominent feature and the audience can see your expressions and visuals, everything else will fade into the background.

Ever notice that no matter

where you are (school, stage, auditorium, conference hall, hotel) the person who knows where the spotlights are or how they work isn't available and no one can find them? Don't let this happen to you. Always ask someone to stand where you'll be standing to make your speech and then get in the audience and make sure the face is lit up. Top lights will black out the face on certain stage locations, and if the audience can't see your face, you're no better than a tape recorder. Move the speaking area into the light or the lights onto the speaker. You want to always be visible and illuminated. You want to get – and keep – the house lights on and up, too. Audiences love to have the lights on, and when they can see each other they're more spontaneous. You can't have too much light.

Dealing with translators/interpreters

As a courtesy to those attending who can't hear, sign language translators are often requested. This service, once a rarity, is now commonplace. I like this because it means everyone can understand and enjoy the presentation. But I do find interpreters distracting on the stage itself because their constant movement can grab the attention of those who don't need a translator. The interpreters can be discreetly placed, and you should arrange this beforehand. If there are going to be translators I find out beforehand and make the

55

necessary arrangements – and often show them where to position themselves.

Check your equipment – and theirs

The importance of being prepared: I was once selected to speak to a group of business students. The presentation consisted of a day of top business people convincing and teaching those juniors and seniors just how fine the business world is. Following an inspiring "how to get a job" lecture, the next speaker, a prominent lawyer representing a large bank, told the students how valuable organization and preparation were, because they saved valuable time. He then introduced the slide show that was the enriching part of his message. The lights went out, but the projector didn't come on. The lights went on, and the projector seemed to be heating up. The lights went out again, but the projector didn't respond. The lights went on again, and "tee hees" and "ho hos" began to ripple across the group. The "prepared" businessman muttered and fiddled with the machine and finally announced there would be a slight intermission at this point. The projector simply hadn't been checked out. Lack of advance preparation let down his presentation.

Make sure the machine or equipment you're counting on to do your demonstrating is working, is charged, is full, is cleaned, is plugged in, is warmed up, etc.

So many times I've seen people grab something off a shelf or out of a suitcase and put it on the podium and when they pick it up to demonstrate, it's empty, it's expired, they can't get the lid off, there's a piece missing.

Always have books marked with pages and pictures found before you stand up. It isn't a sign of intellectual or spiritual bravado to page and thumb through a volume in search of a quote before you start. It's just totally inconsiderate, so have the book open at the place or have the pages reliably marked so that in a half-second you have found it.

Check how the audience is seated

Audiences are made up of individuals, but once grouped together they compound each other, and you actually get a multiplied reaction. For example, a single person will produce, let's say, five units of laughter because he or she is just expressing his or her own spirit and energy as it exists in them. Put two people together and each individual will produce ten units of laughter because the presence of the other person boosts the laughing impulse of each. Get fifty people laughing with or reacting alongside that one person and they'll give even more emotion and energy back to you. (This is why a small crowd can be harder to play to than a large one.)

You always want to seat the audience to encourage this

sure that what is there is neat and orderly. And anything that is distracting can be moved out or covered. Often on stage I pull the curtain and work in front of it. Otherwise the depth of the stage makes you look minute and the backdrop is often shabby or ugly.

• Pay special attention to what's behind you. Lights, movements, ugly drapes, etc. take attention away from you. Don't let anything or anyone distract you.

That seems about right...

"multiplication" effect, so ask your host or hostess beforehand to have everyone seated close together, and at the front. If you're there early, you can make sure this is done. If need be some sections can be roped or ribboned off so the audience is prevented from spreading itself out.

Check your surroundings

Most of the time you cannot change the place or the decor of the place where you are going to speak. You can, however, make

• What is the temperature? Will it be comfortable? There's nothing worse than trying to talk to eight hundred shivering people in an over air-conditioned auditorium, when it's 120°F outside.

• Movement in the room. This is something the audience may not notice, but it can unnerve you. Things like doors open at the back of the room and people going by. Or people sorting things, or handing things out, or counting.

• Watch out for obstructions. I get rid of any and every obstruction I can – even at the head table.

In the face of adversity

You can't ignore adversities in a speaking environment. No matter how carefully you check things beforehand, there'll be problems and you'll have to deal with them whether you like it or not. Ignoring them, even if they aren't your fault, will irritate and distract audiences and take its toll on your attitude and enthusiasm. So tackle them, in four steps:

● **Eliminate**

Because they're there doesn't mean they can't be changed or stopped or that you can't move them – or yourself. Sometimes it takes only five minutes to move to another location and stop the problems. Before you pursue other channels, think elimination.

● **Compensate**

If it won't go away, then get a bigger hammer and flex your biceps and strengthen what you do. I ran across a "perfect" sound system in a beautiful new auditorium that echoed so badly even my family couldn't understand me and thought I was speaking from a cave. Two people with hearing aids got up and left. Finally I ripped off the mike and asked in my normal voice who could and couldn't hear me. I moved the whole audience closer to me and it worked out fine. If need be you can wait for the distraction to go away, or make your presentation longer or shorter, bigger or louder to compensate.

● **Coordinate**

Discuss the problem with the audience. We have a problem here, don't we? What shall we do about it – go on quietly, cry, or complain? Once you make the audience conscious of the problem they become sympathetic and may indeed come up with something that helps, or they may decide, along with you, to just put up with it.

● **Grin and make the best of it**

*Just think of what a great story it'll make when you write **your** book!*

Rules and refresher

★ **Be careful** – *check out everything in advance – the sound system, the lighting, all the equipment for your presentation.*

★ **Be in control** – *eliminate distractions, decline to speak while food is being served, make sure the audience is seated as close together and as close to the front as possible.*

Chapter Six

Just for starters — getting off on the right foot

An audience (even friends, family and lovers) will give you about thirty seconds after you take your place in front of them to convince them that you're worth listening to. If you fail, their physical bodies may remain in place but their mental and emotional energies have gone. Starting your presentation is so critical it's scary – it's a hundred times more important than your ending.

Some friends of mine were once analyzing all the concerts they'd seen in the past five years, discussing the good and the bad. They all concluded that John Denver was the one they liked best. Why? It was simple. After he was announced, he walked out on the stage and entertained and sang. No philosophizing, back-up assistance, bells and whistles – just John Denver. That's what they came to see, and that's what they got. Learn from this that when you speak, get out there and get on with it. People value time and emotion and don't want to wade through previews or preliminaries. They want the beef.

Start on time

Force people to be time conscious. **Remember** if things get off to a late start, meaning you start fifteen minutes late, you'll be blamed for the fifteen-minute overlap. Keep your hosts mindful of it with little remarks and comments if necessary. It helps. Good speakers and speeches are ruined every day by sloppy time schedules. Ask questions like:

"What time is it?" "Is it really 6:30?" "Are we still starting at 8:00?" "Will I really be speaking at 8:15, or is there a possibility I'll be starting later?"

What if your audience is late?

A banker friend of mine speaking on a Sunday morning once had seven people in his audience at

59

starting time and over five hundred by the time he finished. That means 493 ill-mannered people came staggering in during his presentation. This is an outright insult to a speaker. (493 there and 7 tiptoeing in later would be just about tolerable.) If your audience is clearly late in arriving I wouldn't start a talk, but wait – even a half hour if you have to – for the bulk of the group to arrive and ask them to sit at the front.

Remember – you're "speaking" long before you walk up to the stand

So no matter how bad or boring the gathering is (and friends, it can get bad), *pay attention, look interested, laugh, clap, nod* – anything to signal to the audience that you are with them. You're giving a speech long before you stand up and talk. While other speakers and the host were addressing the audience, I saw an important fellow at the head table overhaul his pen, read, adjust his tie and suit lapels, count the dead flies in the lights, clean out his wallet – all in all indicating loud and clear to the audience that he wasn't interested in their meeting, only his talk. This was rude and disrespectful and ultimately hurt him the most. Remember, everyone is sizing you up just before you begin to speak – you just happened to be there before, but now is the hour and, as human nature would have it, everyone is wondering and trying

to anticipate whether you are going to be worth listening to, or had they better get some paper out to read or draw on during your talk. Some tips here:

1. Having your material finished and neatly folded and ready to go (no fumbling).
2. Smile and look anxious to get up and start talking.
3. No fiddling with ties or pens or wallets.
4. Move quickly to the speaking area.

If you listen, you might learn something

You may speak before, between, or after others or you might be the only speaker. In any case, there is always a general purpose to the gathering, something said, done, or presented by others that you pick up on and play off in your presentation. Tying into, supporting, bouncing off, adding to what's going on is called bridging. It's the skill of making yourself a team player instead of a lone wolf message giver. I always try to weave in and build on a point from one of the other speeches or something to do with the main purpose of the gathering. You don't need to repeat, to praise, or to even disagree with anyone who's come before you, you just need to acknowledge the existence of what else is going on. If you listen, you can and will pick up some great seasoning to sprinkle on your speech.

Your introduction – keep it short

If you need a long introduction, you're not worth introducing. The more presentations I gave, the more conscious I became of how bad introductions often were. The more the introduction was made to be funny, cute, poke fun at the speaker or even praise the speaker, the worse it was. I've seen good speakers with a good message annihilated by a fumbling introduction. One night a guy was so slow, we thought he died in the course of the introduction, another tried to outline the speaker's entire topic, another didn't know the speaker and spent ten minutes apologizing for it.

You never want the introduction to attempt to explain your subject or preview any of your material. It only plants preconceived (and possibly erroneous) expectations or prejudices that you'll have to work hard to undo.

Take note of introductions from now on. Most put the speech back about three notches. Once, I did a motivational cleaning seminar to a group of nine hundred women. The group had the material three months beforehand and the woman chosen to introduce me stretched two minutes worth of biographical information into sixteen minutes of droning. Sixteen minutes of introduction – the audience was mentally gone by the time she finished.

Don't let this happen to you.

Don't leave your introduction to chance. No matter how much information I'd send about me beforehand, or how good it was, the organization would lose or confuse it by speech time. I finally decided to take my introductions away from the hosts. Here's what I do now: I write my own tight, one-minute introduction – in the third person – put it on an introduction card and send two cards to my hosts (and carry one with me). Ever since, my introductions have gone well. The only exception is when the hosts insist on reworking it into their own version.

• Be sure you take control of the person introducing you – even to the point of telling them *how,* *when,* and *what* to say. Tease or scare them a little if necessary by telling them if they take too long you might be asleep and they'll have to give the talk – it's called graceful threatening.

• Whoever is introducing you has the job of getting the place calm and organized before presenting you. If there are a lot of empty seats near the front, or people are spread around awkwardly, ask the host to round them up and seat them together. Let the hosts do the dirty work, let them tie up the loose ends and hand you a controlled situation.

As a first step to being a professional speaker, make your own introduction card right now.

61

Introduction Instructions for Don Aslett

The introduction of Mr. Aslett can set the whole mood for the presentation. Please select someone with poise, dignity, and a positive attitude and appearance to handle this. They don't need to try to sell the audience, Mr. Aslett will do that. Make sure the microphone works and everyone can hear *(before starting)*. Please keep Don's introduction short. Don't bog it down with unnecessary extra material. If you want someone "noted" or thanked, hand the information to Mr. Aslett on a card and he will handle it graciously during the presentation. If you have any pre-activities (prayer, pledge, song, sketches, etc.), make sure they come prior to the introduction. It will also be your responsibility to see that *any room activity,* noise or interruptions (catering, eating, furniture moving, etc.), is curtailed during his presentation. Thank you.

Ladies and gentlemen, you are in for a special entertaining, educational and motivational treat – today/or this evening.

Thirty years ago, fresh from a remote Idaho farm, Don Aslett started a cleaning business to pay for his college education. Through inventions, innovations, experience and working sixteen-hour days, his company turned chores and struggles into refined professional techniques. Today, he and his successful company are recognized as leaders of the industry. His writing, speaking, TV appearances and consulting have been employed and enjoyed by thousands of companies and millions of people. He owns and successfully operates several businesses. He is also a bestselling author and TV and media personality.

Don has served on a school board, in the legislature, on many Board of Director assignments, and taught in secondary schools. Don and his wife, Barbara, live on a ranch in Idaho and have six children.

Special notes for special occasions:

And now, as the media has nicknamed him, Billy Graham of the Pine-Sol Set, the Pied Piper of Purification, the King of the Toilet Ring and more, our guest – Mr. Don Aslett.

Hi! I'm Eric Bloodaxe, and this is my friend, Lief the Terrible...

Don't contribute to the thousands of bad introductions given every year. When it's your turn to introduce a speaker, do it well – the way you'd like to be introduced when you give a speech.

• Do it quick – in one to two minutes.

• Avoid stale trite phrases such as: "We are indeed pleased," "It is my delightful pleasure," and "We are here tonight."

• Don't qualify the speaker by predicting the treat that the audience is about to enjoy, or by using flowery statements about the speaker's achievements and qualifications. The speaker can and will show the audience the degree of his or her excellence.

• Don't steal the momentum from the speaker by taking the speaker's time, by previewing the contents of the speaker's talk, trying to get your own message in, or demonstrating what a superior speaker you are. Too many announcers think the audience is there for them.

• If you're introducing someone not known to you personally, interview him or her for a few unhurried moments. Check the pronunciation of the speaker's name. And check the contents of your proposed introduction with the speaker.

• When the speaker finishes, don't sum up, analyze, or try to soften parts of the speech – people know what they heard. Thank him or her graciously and adjourn.

What should you do if you get a bad introduction?

If the person introducing you totally lets you down – and it happens all the time – as you get up, you and the audience will be thinking "What an idiot!" You want the audience to know you didn't like it – because they didn't either. When you get to the front, pause for a minute and look down, then over at the person for a second, and then lower your eyes again. The audience will know you want them to forget what he said and listen to you now. Then start to speak with more power than ever.

Don't try to rescue the introduction unless some flagrant error needs correcting. Or you could ask "Whose introduction card did I give you?" The audience will give you a nervous laugh, then get on with it.

Once you've been introduced, leave it that way

Don't praise and acknowledge the person who gave the introduction – you are the *star,* the one people are here to hear. And don't try to add to the introduction. Don't try to tell people all about who you are or what you know, they'll find it out in a few minutes. Get on with it! Nod and say thank you, skip the list of names and say, "Good evening," or "Hi," or "Hallo," or any greeting you feel comfortable with.

Avoid announcements right at the start

"Before speaking I'd like to make a few announcements" turns off the audience. You've got to giftwrap an announcement if it must be made before or during your talk.

If you want to compliment your hosts or someone in the audience for something, do it somewhere in your speech, not in the opening. Avoid a stiff, deadly formal announcement. "We would like to thank Lonna Jean Tomboy for the souvenir." Instead, the acknowledgement can be cleverly inserted in the body of your talk. You can do it with a question, for example. You can hold up one of the printed schedules of events and say "Did everyone notice how well these were done? I love 'em! Anybody wonder who did such a nice job? – I did, where is she? Susie Sparkle?" The person will raise their hand or stand and the crowd will spontaneously clap. If for some reason you can't thank a person during the course of your speech, you can do it at the end. I do it with a question, like: "Do you always treat toilet cleaners this well? Is your service and hospitality always this good?" Then they say thanks to themselves and really love it. You might also ask them if you can come back and visit or speak again sometime. That in itself says that you like and appreciate them. There's a lot of ways you can express appreciation without using the words "thank you" all of the time.

But if you've got to do it, be creative

If you *must* say thank you at the beginning, there are far better ways to do it than approaching it like a tedious assignment.

For example: A team of people has knocked itself out finding attractive flowers and placing them just so on the tables. Your typical speaker expounds "We would like to thank the fine ladies for the fine flowers to add to this fine occasion." Bad, bad, bad. Yes, acknowledge them, but to do it that way is like kissing your sister

64

– a formality, but far from a thrill. Instead, when you get up to speak, on the way to the stand, stop, smell the flowers and maybe even touch a blossom. Keep your eyes on the flowers as you walk to the front and when you're there ask "Who brought the flowers?" Those flower arrangers will burst their buttons. Ask them to stand and say "Well, we all appreciate them" and lead the applause. This will not only give them a much more genuine and satisfying "thanks," it will also lock you in with the audience because you're including them in the thanks (and besides, who can resist a person who loves flowers!)

Likewise, if you want to make it clear that you are aware and appreciate the fact that a certain person or persons are there, you can do this, too, during your delivery by using them in an example or reference. They'll love it and so will everyone else. I like to do it by mentioning some of the rewards in my life that they've been personally responsible for. That's a great thank-you.

Don't start with a formal greeting

As for the formal greeting or the guest acknowledgement: some call it protocol, I call it awful. "Mayor Jones, Officer Doug, Reverend Mike, Sister Margaret, Honorable Justice Burger, Rin Tin Tin, Visitors, Ladies and Gentlemen (a big breath) ... Good evening!" That's a terrible way to

Friends, Romans, Countrymen, Consuls, Praetors, Quaestors, Tribunes, Lictors, Censors, Centurions...

start a talk. They know who they are and so does everyone else. You aren't there to jibber genealogy – leave out that outdated stuff.

Don't praise or evaluate the speakers before and after you

Don't do it! Let the audience decide for themselves. Standing up behind a loser and trying to patch up his fumbles or apologize in advance for others to come will totally wipe away the audience's respect for you. Leave the analyzing and praising alone – the audience already knows whether your fellow speakers were good or bad, and if they don't agree with your assessment, you've undermined your own credibility. Dabbling in appraisals will be trouble for you either way.

The first minute – how not to start your speech

People start looking you over the minute the introduction begins. By the time it's finished, every eye is on **you**. Have your act together. ● Don't be adjusting your underwear, clipping your nails or talking to someone. ● Never, never, never walk up to the speaker's position with a pile of books and an armful of goodies. That pile of ammunition is as alarming as a police car. Instantly everyone says "oh no!" and they worry more about getting through the material than they do getting through your message. I often use an armful of goods, but I plant them in, around, on, or about the speaking area in advance. ● Don't take food, coffee, etc. to your speaking area, not even water. It's just another thing to distract the audience – they will spend the rest of the speech trying to anticipate when you will reach for it. ● Never fiddle with your personal grooming. Don't adjust your clothes, pick fluff off your outfit, clean your ears or stroke your hair – it looks awkward and is ill-mannered. ● Never carry a briefcase up, open it, and pull out a speech or other material because you'll lose the audience. At most you want a single sheet or notebook in your hand. ● Never walk up to your place and reach in your pocket and pull out a folded speech. ● Never clear your throat when you arrive and face the audience.

Don't review your situation

Many speakers are so fascinated by the fact that they're actually standing in front of the crowd that they spend five minutes telling everyone just how this speech came about. What day it happened, how nervous they were on the way over, how the traffic and weather was this morning, give an appraisal of the meal and the last two speakers, etc. **Nobody cares**. Get on with the message or you are like a plane circling but never landing – people stop watching and waiting.

No sob stories, either

No matter how tough a time you had preparing, finding the place to speak, how many planes were delayed and how many kids you saved on the way in from runaway cars – don't, don't blab it all to the audience. They don't want to know the history of how you got there and why, they only want to hear the message. Reports and analysis of the weather you had to drive through, or how close your connections were and the like is chaff that can smother the wheat germ of your message.

I had a large cleaning concert scheduled in California, once - ι big audience and lots of tickets sold in advance. My props and supplies were shipped in good time so nothing could go wrong and the flight was scheduled to get me in six hours before the 7:00 p.m. starting time. It would take two hours at the most to set up my props, check the sound, etc. Then it turned out that my 11:00 a.m. flight was overbooked and twenty of us were just plain bumped off. I even had a boarding pass! Six airline agents stood by, assuring me they could get me there on the late flight at 9:30 p.m.

A great battle of "You get me there sooner or else" ensued. I won the argument, but there still weren't any flights leaving before 9:30. It was a ten-hour drive by car so it looked like I had no choice but to cancel. By that time I had worked my way to the top of the airlines and they came up with a complicated new routing on another flight from another direction which, with a lot of deep breathing, muttering, praying and running I managed to make. I landed at 6:15 p.m. and the husband of the sponsoring host drove like crazy in a BMW to the large hall. My props were on the stage still in the boxes, and people were coming into the hall. Like a madman I set up the entire stage alone in fifteen minutes. Eight minutes until curtain time, I ran down the hall, showered, shaved, and ran back on to the stage at 7:01 p.m. and did my three-hour show.

How I wanted to weep and tell everyone about this whole afternoon of chaos and how amazing it was that I made it! But they weren't interested in my travel problems or how many meals I

missed; had I recounted my odyssey, ten minutes of their time would have been used up – for what? They knew I was there and that's all they came for, so I just performed. Four or five people there who knew of the dilemmas came up to me after and said, "Wow, nobody knows what a miracle it is that you're here!" That's right, and there was no need for them to know. I had my reward – I was able to do a great job of speaking and entertaining.

Don't put yourself down

The absolute best way to kill a speech (and a lot of speakers do it) is to inform everyone you are a bad speaker. You didn't want to give

67

this talk, you're really no good at this sort of thing. Then make excuses and apologize for the bad job you're going to do.

Never, never apologize or criticize yourself. If you are bad, people will find it out soon enough. No need to tell them now.

Offering humble excuses for your coming presentation is doing nothing less than excusing yourself from the audience's hearts and minds. If you've already told people you're a loser as a speaker, if you do well they're going to think you were putting them on. Remember, no "I'm not worthy of your presence" introductions. You may think it's cushioning you from high expectations, but it's dissolving all expectations.

Start by waiting

It's the very first moment of your speech – they've just introduced you – "And now our main speaker **(you)** ..."

The first thing you do is wait. Whenever there's a change of speaker or events, there's always a few minutes for the audience to twitch, wriggle, chew a mint, adjust their skirts or ties, run to the restroom, etc., and so a minor turmoil is going on. It'll die down if you give it a second or two. Overanxious speakers start talking the minute they hit the podium – don't do it! Don't begin your delivery while the audience is still shuffling around and settling in. You can gain more psychological and emotional audience control by a few seconds of waiting at the beginning than in an hour of dynamism during your delivery. Take your place, give the audience a sweeping look, spanning everyone in front and behind as if to say "Are you ready?" The longer you stay quiet, the quieter they get. **Wait**, don't try to drown them out, ride with the noise if you have to. Waiting five seconds will seem like five minutes, but that's OK, you can take it. When all is quiet (it may even take a glare at the dish rattlers), **begin**.

Rules and refresher

★ *Be aware – take note of what else is going on, who else is speaking and remember that you are being watched even when you're not actually talking.*

★ *Be assertive – avoid announcements and apologies and long-winded explanations. Make sure you're introduced properly and then make your presentation.*

Chapter Seven

Delivering the goods

All successful people in any field – mechanics, sports, teaching, etc. – mentally and emotionally bleed for what they're doing, if they're any good. You as a speaker must do the same – give all of your heart, mind and strength – all your energy, not part of it. What happens then is automatic – the audience in return will give the same thing back to you. You'll trade pint for pint and never give it a second thought. And though I'm drained at the end of every speech, I always feel I came out ahead.

I am and always have been a hands-on, pick-and-shovel, right-in-the-field worker. I mean real hard cement-laying, beam-lifting jobs, in construction and on the farm, but speaking is by far the hardest job I've ever done. A one-hour performance can leave me like a limp dish rag. In fact, you can use this as a measure of your performance: if you're exhausted at the end of it, you're on the road to success (unless it's from dodging missiles!)

Remember: Your position or experience doesn't guarantee results. Each delivery stands on its own – you make it stand.

Your delivery and your voice

Whether it's hoarse or sweet, use your own voice and your own expressions. Sincerity is the all-time best way to get a message across. Quaking, quivering, sniffling, whispering in oratorical emotion is for actors, not for a professional speaker. Don't hype your voice or yodel out syllables, rolling your eyes and tongue. Make your voice louder or softer, quicken it or slow it down for good communication, but never roll out the "holy" quake. Most people are used to a little quaking as part of a preacher's style, but they won't put up with it from you. Trying to emphasize a grave point with a fake quake will cause the audience to quiver in disgust.

The old "choked-up" routine, too, if faked, can turn off the audience. Tears can have incredible impact if they're real. If you try to conjure them up, they'll wash you out. All intelligent people recognize emotion by its feel, not its sound. You only fool the ones too dumb to know true emotion, so you're wasting your breath.

Keep it lively

Vary your delivery. Change your tone of voice, lower and raise your voice, use a short sentence after several long sentences. Ask a few questions, even just rhetorical questions. At all costs, avoid a monotonous, flat, even presentation – you could have the most interesting speech in the world, but if your delivery is boring, the audience will never know it.

Speed of delivery – fast vs. slow talking

Speaking a little faster than usual certainly beats talking too slow. Fast-paced talking requires keener listening and will make the audience pay more attention. It also gives them the subliminal message that this speech is not going to go on all day and all night. You don't want to sound like an auctioneer, but pick up the pace a little more than your regular conversational speech. Talking too fast is the biggest complaint I get

– especially from the elderly. But the majority like the machine-gun fire approach that I use, so I just make sure I slow down for older audiences. (But make sure that when you do slow down, you don't talk down!)

Another benefit of a fast-paced dialogue is that when you do slow down, or stop dead, the audience is alerted to the fact that "this must be important." It's a great way to emphasize.

The virtues of sincerity

People will surely one day forget most of what you said, but few will forget how you said it. You'll notice this book contains little technical instruction on speaking. The reason is simple – most of you don't need it, because you are what you are. Your own speaking style may be quite different, or even a little odd or strange, but your natural approach will be

He's all heart!

superior – for you – to any "common standard" speaking technique. Experience will shape and develop your own technique quickly. You'll end up sincere and effective if you just be yourself. Over-rehearsed and over-polished speakers are often so smooth that their presentations run past their listeners, without making a dent. A bad presentation delivered sincerely will be more effective than a brilliant one delivered falsely.

Avoid gushiness

"You're the greatest people and I love you all...." If someone doesn't know us and says that to us right away, we aren't likely to love them or think they're the greatest speaker. Compliments are great if sincere. But insincere compliments aren't just neutral – they rip away the whole foundation of belief in your message. Gushiness is something only a young, sweet, innocent couple can get away with, otherwise it just comes out sickening.

Don't just stand there talking – move!

Movement and action carry a message as well as words. Voice or movement alone have limitations, but voice with action gets attention. It teaches and changes lives.

A clenched fist, half-closed eyes, a cocked head, raised eyebrows, a bowed head, or a stomping foot can turn a simple word into a powerful active statement – make people sweat, cry, laugh or flinch. Movements you make while you're speaking are called gestures. Most gestures are natural and instinctive and we all use them in our conversations and entreaties and discussions and arguments. But once in front of a crowd, we often look as if we've been transformed into a stick, and try to give a speech with our mouth alone.

She froze again!

A good speaker uses every part of his or her body. For example, you can look straight at the audience and say in a speech, "the voters said **yes** to the proposal," and everyone will understand. Say the same thing while nodding your head affirmatively and everyone will not only understand, they'll nod with you and remember.

Be a mover, but not a pacer

It might relax you to pace and weave around in front of people,

71

but it doesn't do much for your observers. If body movement strengthens or improves communication, use it. If it's more like a way to exercise in public, lose it. I did a simple thirty-second commercial for a chemical company and we had to re-shoot it more than twenty times, mostly because I "weaved" about like a birch tree in the wind. Things like this may be natural mannerisms, but as a speaker you don't want to be *totally* natural. When and if you move, do it deliberately and quickly. Don't move without purpose – it's irritating and unnerving. Re-position yourself if you must, but don't sway and rove.

Hands, not fingers

Another little thing that too many people do is use their fingers in all sorts of grotesque positions – bent and crooked, like they're performing using some bizarre sign language. Hands, not fingers, are good for the audience to look at.

The audience can't see finger movements clearly when you're fifty feet away from them.

Watch those awkward little mannerisms

The more you speak, the more aware you'll become of other speakers and all their little mannerisms that bother you, the more you will correct in yourself. I once saw a guy who leaned on everything – he drove me crazy. Then I realized that once in a while, I leaned too. So I stopped – it was easy. If you see a speaker fiddling with his glasses, constantly putting them on and taking them off – you'll stop. It'll be the same with pacing, looking down at your outline too much, etc. But don't get too uptight about your little eccentricities, they'll go away with experience as you begin to imitate the things you do like in others and discontinue the things you don't like. It does, of course, help to ask people's opinion – get their objective appraisal of you. Just don't weep or hate them when they tell you how gross you look licking your lips between every sentence.

Make sure you can be seen as well as heard

Being seen is the first principle of effective speaking, it even comes before being heard! And this means you want that audience to be able to see all of you – from your head down to your little toes.

Always speak from an elevation if at all possible. If not, spread or circle the people around close enough to you so that they can see you, even at floor level. When I speak on floor or audience level, I often keep an empty chair close by so that when I'm showing or demonstrating something, I can jump up on the chair. Audiences appreciate it when you let them know you care whether or not they can see.

And that means getting out from behind that podium!

Never, never allow yourself to be put behind a "stand." They might just as well lock you in a box and punch some air holes for your voice to come out. If there's a stand, I take the mike off it and move it out of the way or get in front of it. You can't communicate from behind things, it's rude as well as ineffective. I've seen very good people (who happened to be short) with a good message lose audiences, sales and elections because only their forehead or hair was showing.

Look at this:

Which appeals? Which communicates? How could anyone even conceive of delivering a message behind a big block of wood with only their neck and head showing? You don't speak with just your head and a few white knuckles (which is about all that shows beyond a podium), **you speak with your whole body**.

Keep up the pace

Speaking is conversation – *condensed*. Don't waste time, and don't get bogged down in trivia! Keep the energy flowing.

Some of the greatest training I ever had in improving my speaking came when I began doing television. Previously I thought I had lots of time to build into and out of stories, so I was throwing in and getting away with a lot of not-strictly-pertinent things. I didn't generally worry much about being inefficient with my time in front of an audience and thus had a lot of wasted words and material. Then I tried to tell an involved story on a four-minute news slot. It was an awakening experience. There was no time to fiddle and

build an elaborate frame around the message. I had to work out very carefully beforehand what I wanted to get across, think of a snappy opening (for example, condensing the usual speech opening from five minutes to thirty seconds), get into the meat of the subject, convince people of what I wanted to convince them and then sum it up. All in four minutes or less! From then on, things I used to take a half hour to teach and tell, I was doing in five minutes.

Although speaking is basically the same as daily conversation, you do have to condense it. For some reason, audiences can absorb information faster than an individual alone – it must be all the psychic energy in the air, or maybe somehow they help each other. So don't drag it out, always try to increase your normal speed of delivery a little (it gives you

more electricity and zap as a speaker) and throw out the information you don't need. Think of it as going on a hike across the mountains. You're just trying to get to the other side and enjoy the walk, and anything extra you carry along the way will only distract from that goal. It's the same with speaking – condense!

Keep track of where you are

You do want to keep track of where you are, but never want to be caught looking at your watch, or everybody will glance at their watches too!

I do two things to keep the audience from knowing I'm keeping track of the time: first, I wear my wristwatch on the palm side of my wrist so that when I gesture or do something with my hand, I can see the time without pulling up my sleeve or using the old cocked arm routine. Second, I find the clock in the room and make sure it's accurate. If I'm right on target or close to the times noted on my outline, I just roll on. If I'm out by a mile, then I quickly calculate what I have to cut short or fill in with. If you have doubts about the length of your speech, cut it shorter.

You'll also become an expert at reading the audience. When they glance at their watches and roll their eyes to the ceiling, fall asleep, start reading or writing, it's a pretty strong indication that you're finished. Also, remember that no matter how good you are, or how compelling your subject, if they've had a full day of classes, lectures, projects, etc., before you then you're starting out with a big handicap. It does happen, so appraise the situation before you speak and keep an eye on their alertness and stop when they begin to wilt, even if you have ten more dynamite stories to tell. They'll ask you back again and again – crowds love short and to the point speakers.

Stand ready to adjust your speech

There are an infinite number of things that can happen before or during your speech that might influence what you say and how long you take. This is no cause for alarm, but it is something you should be aware of so you can be ready to make adjustments and be flexible.

Situations that call for you to adjust to what's happening are many.

- the presentation may be running too long or too short
- the air conditioner may go haywire and everyone is gasping for breath
- one of the other speakers may be incredibly bad or good
- there may be an announcement that has life-changing significance
- you may end up in prime-time competition with the World Golf Series or some other popular event.

On one occasion the woman before me really botched the job of speaking to six hundred youths on the subject of interviews and resumés. I mean she was bad – and she was a big name too. I shifted my talk around a little, gracefully tracked back to the subject of resumés, added on to what she'd said and summed it all up so the students couldn't fail to understand it. Then I thanked her for getting the ball rolling on such an important subject, and such a

good one to lead in with. At the end, the students gave me a standing ovation and she graciously (knowing she blew it) thanked me. We all benefited.

Don't go on and on

The length of your talk: Wow, does it make a difference. Actually, it's a lot like cooking – you have to turn the heat down at precisely the right time. If you turn it off too soon, the food is raw and undigestible, but if you go over, even a minute or two on some things, it's tough, burned and unpalatable.

Be careful about long drawn-out thank-yous and appreciation sessions. Even these, nice as they are, can begin to erode the basic drama of your appearances. Try to go for one clean chop and sit down. If they clap and cheer for you to stand up again, do so and try to say something short and funny but "conclusive" such as "Well, thank you again! I'm speaking in France tomorrow, can I take you with me?" (Believe it or not one lady believed my offer and I got an irate letter from her

husband, who didn't think taking his wife to France as a portable audience was such a good idea!)

A double dose ruins the best of anything: sleep, play, food, visits etc. We enjoy each of these until they're overdone. A common tendency for speakers – when an audience is fresh, enjoys the message and rewards the speaker with thunderous applause – is to take

Rules and refresher

★ **Be natural** – move while you speak, use gestures, vary your delivery – just as you would when telling a story to friends at the office. Don't, under any circumstances, become a talking head droning on from behind a podium.

★ **Be flexible** – don't, whatever you do, punish the audience with a long speech at the end of a long evening. If everyone's tired and it's getting late – cut it short.

that as "they must want more." So they overspeak, overdo, overkill. I admit it's a tough judgement to make but you do have to remember that you've been projecting and emoting and moving around on stage – the exact opposite of what the audience has been doing, sitting attentively.

Enough is enough – know the audience, know their capacity.

Remember – it's not all you

Even if you're the main speaker, have your name in the biggest type and your picture on the poster, even if you prepare, worry, and stew over your speech for six months ahead – even get paid more than anyone else – the presentation isn't all you – almost every assembly of people called together has:

- *Announcements*
- *Awards*
- *Introductions*
- *Reports*
- *Recognitions, etc.*

Activities like these surround your presentation and even if these preliminaries cut into your time (which they will, 90% of the time), don't get "huhu" (Hawaiian for angry and put out) – just budget your time and become an even more effective speaker. Don't ever decide to get even and make the audience sit and listen to your entire speech no matter how late it is – if necessary condense down to the best of your message and make them bawl and beg for more next time.

Your worst fears

You'll never get rid of stage fright completely. And that's a good thing, because part of stage fright is the building tension and excitement crucial to an outstanding presentation. A little fear and respect, a tinge of terror is actually good for your delivery. It helps you concentrate and focus on your speech, it helps you to be more aware of the audience's mood and the mood of the occasion. But you don't want to be overwhelmed by stage fright. So it's worth considering what it is you're really afraid of, and how to control that fear.

The mass of beady eyes

I handle my fear of the audience by standing outside the building or speaking area twenty minutes before my talk. As the people arrive I help direct them in, or strike up a conversation with them, "Where are you from? Why did you come?" etc. I give some of them a free book or little souvenir. Boy, does this help – I rediscover the fact that they're just people

like me and you, they're friendly and anxious to learn, and they are coming full of respect and regard for me. I also come to feel that I actually know a lot of them (and I note a few of the names to address during my presentation). Best of all, I know those people will go in there and "show and tell" everyone sitting within thirty feet of them, what a kind and interesting person the speaker is!

Fainting

The secret fear of many speakers and would-be speakers who have experienced that old rapid heartbeat, is that they are going to get up in front of the audience and faint dead away. Now have you ever seen – or even heard of anyone who's seen – anyone faint from fear in front of an audience? I did know of someone who was talking and preaching away in church, and died on the spot standing up. The audience saw him go, he suddenly stood there and then fell to the floor dead as a match. He was ninety-three. If you're under eighty-five, your chance of surviving a speech, or making it through fully conscious, is around 100%.

Dry throat

Who can explain it? But it happens to everyone, even to me, in about one out of every forty speeches. Your mouth turns dry and you're sure someone slipped in a spoonful of alum. Most of this is psychological. The audience will never be aware of it. No dust will come out of your mouth and the dryness will pass quickly. I had a real struggle with it until my speech professor told me that no one notices it, then it never bothered me again. It helps a little to always drink water before you start. But it's uncouth to drink while you're speaking – the audience will think you're tanking up for another hour at the podium and the very thought of it will turn them off.

Nobody comes

It happens – I once rented a thousand seats, advertized on a major TV show, put up posters and handed out announcements, and only two people came. Another time I made similar elaborate preparations and only eight came. But I did the whole show and came out alive. Getting hung up with how many come is all ego – let's face it!

Sometimes, because of a lower-than-expected attendance, seeing all those empty chairs, a speaker feels irritated and "punishes" the audience, expressing his disappointment publicly, even cutting his talk short. This is totally unprofessional. You can't blame those who came for those who didn't. If even one person shows up, if you're a professional you'll treat him or her like the thousands you expected to be there.

Too many people come

Too big a crowd can be a more serious problem than too little. We had seats for 380 once and 790 people turned up. They ended up pushing, shoving, and yelling obscenities at me because they couldn't hear. No matter how well-designed an auditorium or hall is, when crowds exceed seven hundred the rest of those people will be sitting more than sixty feet from you. Your facial expressions (and many of your visual aids) are totally lost on them. When I know beforehand that the crowd is going to be very large, I prepare larger visual aids. Often in a big crowd I pass around the things I'm talking about and constantly refer to and talk to the people "in the back." That brings them in and makes them feel more a part of the seminar or speech. Big audiences also take longer to get in and settle down, and their laughter is longer, so generally your speech will run 5 to 10% longer – remember that.

You go blank

Sometimes when I'm rolling along at a high rate of speed I think a minute ahead of where I am and lose my train of thought. I mean, I go blank! Whenever this happened during a speech my solution used to be to pick a new point and start again. But I felt like an utter idiot. I handled the problem this way for years until one day, listening to a well known speaker I admired, I saw it happen to him. I blushed for him as he groped to remember what he was pursuing. He looked straight at us and said, "I lost my train of thought – where was I?"

Fifty of us in the audience who all knew the feeling leaped forth with the information. He smiled, thanked us graciously, and continued. We loved him for that. He let us help him and he admitted he was an occasionally absent-minded human like the rest of us. A quick glance at your little outline should also help reassemble your train of thought. But don't fret too much over these lapses, everyone in the audience has had it happen to them.

Foot-in-mouth mistakes

If you have any gravel in your guts as a speaker, you're going to have a slip of the lip from time to time or, as some say, be hung by your tongue. It happens to the best of us. You handle foot-in-mouth mistakes by leaving the foot right there and continuing your talk. To try to correct or amend it just draws more attention to it and 95% of the time you dig yourself in deeper. It will happen; you'll be expounding on the shame of going to prison, suddenly the face of a mother whose son is in prison will stand out of the audience. You want to die of embarrassment – **don't**. You two are the only ones affected. Leave it that way.

human you appear to the audience, the better you'll communicate. If you goof (and you will), don't panic, don't live in fear of it.

Going through my well-polished cleaning demonstrations (in a three-piece suit), I occasionally kick over a bucket, slip on water, or miss a step. I've learned to stop and give everyone time to laugh. Then I laugh and go on.

Audiences want to laugh, cry or help correct with you. In fact, most goofs will be a plus for you, to the point that some speakers obviously fake and plan a "problem." Audiences are usually so compassionate they still like it, even if they know it was staged.

You make a goof

When you do a stupid thing, everything isn't lost – the more

80

Chapter Eight

Show and tell

Too many people think visual aids are an option, a standby for speaking. Not so. Visual aids are so important in a presentation that I won't address a subject if I can't use them. Good visual aids/props are one of the axles of your speech vehicle. As the famous old expression goes: "a picture is worth a thousand words." Showing something will save a lot of time trying to talk about it or describe it. It also adds another dimension to **you**. An action, like holding something and demonstrating it as you talk, can vastly improve your effectiveness and your power of persuasion. A visual – even the simplest one – talks to an audience and eliminates the need for the audience to rely on their imagination. Speaking is more than words coming out of your mouth – speaking is communicating, inspiring, motivating, teaching. It calls for every trick at your command, and visuals are your magic hat.

Share the burden

When you have visuals (any physical item that goes on stage with you), it does a lot to build your confidence. You aren't alone! The whole burden of the job isn't on you. You have help, a tool, a toy, a chart, a companion to take people's eyes off you for a second and share the speech. Always use as many visual aids as you possibly can without overpowering the audience.

Teach by experience

In school the instructor talks, shows visuals, asks the student to read, asks him or her to write down notes, and to do a quiz. Each of these mediums repeats and reinforces the message in the student's mind, to help him or her absorb as much of the information as possible. The more of an "experience" you can give your audience with the subject, the more it'll stick in their mind and be remembered.

Let's take an example: In my professional lectures, I often presented prevention as the number one way to keep homes and buildings clean. In telling the audience that door mats really did save work, I used only words at first to describe door mats and their uses and benefits. I got no response. One day I was describing the mats in my cleaning supplies store, and I referred to the ones at the back of the room – every head turned, so I brought a mat on stage. People liked that even better. Then one day as I was describing what a mat does, I asked them to feel the grit that was hanging on the bottom of their shoes. They murmured in astonishment, and **they** were my visual aids. A few months later my presentation was so dynamic I thought it couldn't improve. Now I was even passing a sample mat through the audience as I spoke, but the winning, crowning visual aid was again not a thing, but an action. I often told my audiences not to pick flashy monogrammed or elaborately decorated mats because people wouldn't clean their feet on them – again, in words that few remembered. One day I walked up to a heavily-decorated mat and said, "Now if you pick too plush or too pretty a mat, do you know what people will do?" Then I took a giant leap over the mat. Everyone loved it and cheered and bought mats.

Visual aids aren't just objects

A gesture or action or demonstration can be a visual aid, too. Let's give a talk to a group of teenagers who were brought up in strict homes cut off from the world and teach them what a kiss is:

Words – We describe a kiss (it sounds silly).

Sound – We make the sound of a kiss, but to them it sounds like a cow pulling its leg out of the mud, and they laugh.

Sight – We pucker our lips and show the proper form. They think we just sucked a lemon and giggle.

Sight and sound – We then kiss the air with a loud smack and they think we're licking our chops for lunch.

Simulated experience – We have them kiss the air or the back of their hand and explain further with words, now that they know the mechanics.

Actual experience – We get a couple of very handsome boys and girls as assistants who go into the audience and kiss to show exactly what's involved.

Though it wasn't an object, we used a visual aid and the lights sure came on.

YOUR MESSAGE

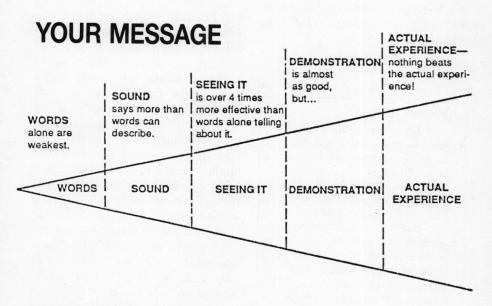

Special effects

What are often called "special effects" (fireworks, animals, trick objects, etc.) are just the more dramatic kind of visual aid. I'd bring an elephant on stage if it would help the audience learn, enjoy or understand my presentation. I remember one army instructor lecturing on the danger and use of firearms to a five hundred student class outdoors. He not only brought the guns and rifles he was talking about on stage, he loaded one with full powder and used wadded-up newspaper for the lead and fired it right into our group. We understood perfectly what he was saying and the kids on whose heads the bits of charred newspaper fell still haven't forgotten that lesson.

Don't go overboard

Be effective, but be careful. And make sure your message and delivery are strong enough to stand up against your special effect. Here's a perfect example of failing to do this: At a graduation talk a red-headed graduate stood up to give her address. "On your mark, get set, GO!" as she drew out a starter's pistol, and fired it into the air. As you might imagine she had the instant and full attention of everyone. But her ammunition was spent – the talk that followed was weak and quaint compared to the big bang start, and she lost not only her audience but her effectiveness, too.

Use paper, not blackboards

For writing as you speak, giant white pads of paper are better than blackboards. Blackboards are a whole can of worms in themselves: you have to find the chalk/erasers, take time to erase, worry about running into waxy spots that won't take chalk, or soft finishes from which chalk can't be completely erased, getting chalk all over your clothes/hands/nose, and dropping and breaking the chalk. And blackboards often have a glare that makes the board unreadable to some parts of the audience.

White paper gives you variety – so you're not stuck with black and white – and the markers you use can be bright and fresh. You've probably seen, or may own a "white board" that uses erasable felt markers – any other markers won't come off! You'll need cloth to "erase" the board, and after many uses it needs to be cleaned thoroughly with a liquid cleaner available where white boards are sold. A white board can present a glare problem, so check this possibility out before the show.

Keep your visuals invisible – till their moment comes

It's important to hide visual aids from the audience's view, behind a curtain or under a podium, so no one can see them, then pull them out as they're called for in your speech. The element of surprise is a plus for your presentation and providing the audience with something new to look at from time to time will do a lot to hold their interest.

Timing and visuals

Remember, visuals will make your speech run much longer than if you were giving it without visuals. So don't time your speech from the outline and then add the visuals later. If you know you'll be using visuals, run through the entire presentation beforehand, and time it accordingly. Failing that, calculate an additional two to five minutes per slide.

Visuals are just aids

Yes, visuals can greatly enhance a speech – but they can't replace the speech. No matter how many visuals you plan to use, you must still be able to give the speech – powerfully as ever – without them. Accidents will happen – electricity fails, machines break down – and you'll still have to talk. So don't think you can skip making an outline just because you've got some terrific slides – the speech is always the most important part of a presentation.

Don't forget the audience

Too often speakers spend half their time talking to the visuals instead of the audience. Face forward as much as possible. Point with the arm nearest the screen or pad so that you're not twisting around in front of what everyone's trying to see. If necessary have a copy of the visual in front of you so that you can read or describe it without having to turn your back on the audience (see the visual reproduced on my sample outline, page 37). And please, please make sure that everyone can see. If you haven't checked out sight lines before the start, don't fail to do so with the first slide.

Visual aid accidents

Most visual aid problems can be avoided by simply taking the few minutes or seconds necessary to put things through their paces in advance. If there are any doubts, you'd better have a standby or at least a great comeback line to cover yourself with the audience!

- out of focus
- upside down
- wrong speed
- burnt-out bulb
- wrong format
- no outlet

Nothing is worse than a foul-up with an audience. As you scratch your way across giant note pads with a nearly-dried-up felt marker, believe me, you're getting boos and hisses in the minds of onlookers. An overhead projector at the wrong angle will literally be a pain in the neck for the audience. Time and again presentations are turned from special to a spectacle because someone failed to check it out. Make sure your slides are in the correct sequence and loaded properly. If you're using their slide projector, your slides will have to be marked in the lower right-hand corner so that it's obvious in an instant what way round they should be. Pre-run whenever you can, or at least prepare a plan to fall back on. If you're supplying the projector, bring some spare bulbs just in case. A machine that won't work is just as bad, or worse, than a totally silent speaker. Know your machine, check your machine, have the slide or overhead projector out and ready and in order.

And never, never, search for, or sort, your visual aids in front of a group or your presentation is finished. If you can't find it, they can't find room to hear it.

To hand out or not to hand out

Why hand-outs are useful

1. They give the audience a little present, free information that people can easily use later in the conference or in everyday life.

2. They save the distraction of people digging for pens and paper, trying to take notes and asking "What did he say?"

3. Hand-outs can also save you from being mobbed with questions or requests for your business cards, etc.

Why hand-outs are a pain in the neck

Give someone sitting down something to rattle, rip or read, and that's exactly what they'll do, right while you're trying to get their undivided attention.

How and when to give a hand-out

Not while you're talking.
- Never give a hand-out before or during your speech, unless it'll be used or needed in the presentation.
- Don't stop a presentation for hand-outs.

Use break time.
- Distribute things while everyone is "out", and when they return everyone can dive into the material as you dive into the subject.

The pile and pass method.
- Another way is to count tables or rows and plant as many piles as you need against the wall or under the table, and when the hand-out is needed say something like, "Each of you reach down to your right." In ten seconds everyone has the material and you can hold the flow. Never break a sentence.

On their way out. Give anything you do want to give out at the end if possible. After you've finished, that is, not while you're finishing.
- You can hold up a hand-out, show it and let everyone see it and then point at the door or side of the stage and tell everyone to pick one up on their way out.
- Staple, clip or otherwise bind your hand-out. Then it will be quiet, contained, and easily usable. Constant handling and shuffling of loose pages will disrupt you and disgust the audience.

Transporting visuals

You can carry your visual aids with you or get or improvise them at the place you're speaking. But if you have a trunkload of special props that are a vital part of your show (perhaps you're a magician, or your presentation like my "cleaning concerts" depends on objects and materials that aren't easy to come by everywhere), somehow they must travel with you. It'll do you no good to arrive on the appointed day only to have the carrier say "It'll only be a day's wait to get your shipment back."

For years I shipped my props with me on the plane. That sounds safe, but many times I showed up, while the props didn't – and I didn't have a show. I even learned to allow extra hours to be sure and allow time for baggage transfer. But a few years ago I discovered an easier way: I bought a trunk that holds fifty pounds, I loaded it up, and used a parcel service to ship it in advance allowing five extra days beyond how long they said it would take to get there, to allow for disasters and mistakes. It's cheap and often the sponsor pays for the shipping. It saves a lot of heave-hoing, suit-snagging, worrying and waiting at airports.

Throwing things into the audience

Sometimes this makes a hit, other times it hits someone. If it's done quickly and to the right groups, throwing something into the audience is fun, and it gets them involved and wakes them up. But give a little thought to the item and the group – hitting a senior citizen on the head with a frisbee won't impress anyone. If you have even a wink of doubt, walk down and hand it to someone and ask them to pass it back, or put it on the counter and invite someone up later to get it.

Rules and refresher

* **Be daring** – visuals are fun, useful, instructive – give them a try.
* **Be sensible** – don't make your visuals more interesting than your speech – and make sure any visuals are ready to go and in working order way ahead of the presentation time.

Chapter Nine

"A" is for Audience

When you're turned on to the audience, the audience is turned on to you. And just as you can regulate a sound or heat level with a knob, you can and will regulate your audience.

Audiences have been described as good, lively, cooperative, bad, dead, unresponsive, suspicious, and conservative – not so. Audiences are people, in different moods, at different times, but it's *you* who determine the quality of your audience.

I promise that if you are prepared, you'll have no fear of your audience, and they'll give to you, not take away. Treat them like an intimate friend, not a shapeless mass, and watch how they melt to your side.

Eye contact

Be sure to always give the "eye" to those you talk to. Like a hawk on a hungry hunting morning, hold your head up and look deep into the faces and eyes of those listening to you.

I had speech training at school and I knew the mechanical way to make "eye contact," to make everyone in the room think I was talking to them individually, but no one ever told me to look at the

faces too. I'd become so concerned with putting on a good show I related to the audience as a "group" or mass.

One evening I was reviewing a video of a seminar I did that was taped by a television company. Sometimes the cameraman would pan the audience's faces while my voice was going on on stage. Some of those faces had a look of complete joy, almost an hypnotic state of appreciation, they were hanging on every word I said, their eyes moving to catch every movement. It was frightening but also motivating. From then on I started really looking at the people, and their presence, kindness, and interest was like an inspiration and motivation to deliver the best I could. Really look at those you are speaking to! That's simple enough and it'll take care of eighty-three pages of philosophy, technique, and instruction on speaking.

Where are those faces?

How the audience is seated relative to you is critical. If they're too far away, behind something, or squeezed into a prenatal position, it cramps their concentration and blocks communication. Comfort is essential to absorption and again, as the speaker, you are in control.

A highly formal setting often holds people in a formal mood. I break this up when I can, seating the audience, and speaking, in the place that's most conducive to the

audience seeing and hearing me well.

On the other hand, things can get *too* informal. An audience seated in an auditorium will be 30% more attentive than one seated at conference tables where they can clink ice, rattle tea cups, sort papers, twist paper clips, etc. And talking to an audience sprawled out on the grass or on the beach provides the opportunity to sleep – they can all snooze or chase bugs or throw pebbles or pick flowers, in addition to all the usual distractions, rather than listen to you. Don't give your audience too much room to play in.

Everyone, face the front

If you're speaking at a banquet or dinner, half of the audience will have their backs to you. If the host hasn't already asked, suggest that they turn their chairs away from the tables and face the front. Make sure you give them enough time to shift their chairs and settle in before you begin to speak. There's no way you can have eye contact with an audience if half of it has to crane their necks around and look over their shoulders just to see and hear what's going on. And believe me, if they're uncomfortable, you soon will be too.

Watch out for the old side view

If the audience is too far to the sides, you'll have a very hard time getting eye contact. In fact, you're very likely to begin to talk to one side more than the other. I've had people yell out of the audience, "Hey, Don, what about this side?" Sometimes at dinners or other occasions with "U" shaped seating, you can end up with part of the audience behind you. Avoid this if possible. If not, be aware of the situation and make sure you look at, move to and gesture to both sides. Do the same with parts of your audience seated in a balcony. This is difficult, since looking up often isn't in our habits or training, but the people in the balcony will otherwise see plainly by your head and gestures that they're not included.

Get the audience close to you

Proximity does a lot to increase your effectiveness. I like the audience five feet in front of me. I know I mentioned this in the chapter on setting up, but it's so important

to your success with an audience that I'm saying it again. You want to get close to people, so they can feel your moves as well as see them. You shouldn't accept a spot to speak from if it cuts you off from the audience. Often I'll get off the stage and walk up till I'm just two or three feet from the audience. Or I take ten rows of chairs (before the speech, obviously) out of the back and move them up in front of the first row of chairs until they're three feet from the stage. I like the host or presiding person to pull the audience together, but if they won't do it, I do it myself. Tight groups radiate compatibility and they make your message a lot easier to deliver.

Speak to the individual

There's no such thing as "group communication." You never speak to a "group" or a mass, only to individuals. You are talking to

each individual person when you stand in front of an audience, whether it's 2,500 or two million. If you speak just to "the mass," people know it. They feel it and you don't get in touch with any of them. It's like the hunter (man or mountain lion) that goes after prey and runs into a whole massive herd of what he was after. It would seem like a "can't miss" opportunity, yet if either of the hunters "flock shoot" or "flock chase," they always miss.

The successful speaker, like the successful hunter, picks out an individual and addresses that person, no matter what the distractions are. When I stand in front of an audience, I always remind myself, "I'm not here to make money, impress the media, or get applause, I'm here solely to enrich, enhance, teach, and inspire individuals" and so I talk to each of them, the grandmother, the daughter, the son, the father, the brothers, the discouraged, the eager. I rally every drop of energy I have and talk, plead and use logic on each and every person.

I never see an audience as a group or band, I see and address each single seat, as if each one were the only one there, the only important one.

The one-to-one flow

If you address each single person, they relate back to you which creates a one-to-one flow, within which you can dramatize and produce emotion. This is what holds an audience.

Let me give an example of exactly how this is done. Let's say that 450 people are waiting for you, a great expert professional cleaner, to speak. They've just introduced you. Loud applause rises from these 450 individuals, all with their individual cleaning problems, all there for individual help and inspiration.

Standard:
"Hello, I'm very happy to be with you all tonight, and I have some great tips for you. I love your beautiful city, your weather and this lovely hall."

Magic:
"Well ... How did your house

look when you left? [Each person in the audience is instantly involved and challenged.] OK ... instead of listening to this for two hours, who would rather have me clean their house?"[I've touched on the audience's true emotions and made another very direct one-to-one statement.]

(You're pointing to one or two individuals) "Those of you who think you hate cleaning now are going to be so good and fast at it before we're finished that you'll start your own company."

When we have a one-on-one conversation in everyday life, we learn pretty fast that if we take over and use up all the time, do all the talking and decision making, etc., it isn't long until people avoid us. So to get listened to, we learn to listen and we give our "audience" some time to have a say and participate, too.

Yet when we speak to a group, we have a tendency to think "Oh, now it's all me, I can give all my thoughts and feelings and message." Wrong! You're still talking to an individual and they still need to be part of it. Let them have it and you'll always capture and control your audiences.

> *People may forget what you said, but they will never forget how you made them feel.*

Let your audience tell you how you're doing

Like a good salesman you have to watch the audience and let them tell you whether you're getting the job done or not. Heads nodding up and down or dropped down in a doze will tell you whether they're asleep or listening to you.

I constantly question the audience about the subject, a lot of rhetorical questions – nothing formal, very little hand raising. But, after I describe the good or the bad of something I will throw it back at the audience. Sometimes it's just leaning towards them and

Rules and refresher
* ★ *Get the audience close* – *the closer the better.*
* ★ *Get them together* – *if they're spread everywhere, pull them in close. An audience close together reinforces itself and is a lot more confident and spontaneous.*

gesturing and sometimes its actually handing them something and saying: "Here, who wants this?" If I've done a decent job they'll either reach, raise their hands, or yell for it – or all be silent and draw back in horror! Remember the audience is why you are there so work with them, use them, ask them, give to them. Quite honestly, some of my funniest experiences have come from calling on members of the audience and I've incorporated some of those wild audience responses into my presentations.

Repeat audience comments

Remember that you and the audience are one. When a question or comment is made from the audience, often from the front row, and you respond brilliantly, everyone will hear *you* because you have a microphone, but generally those at the back of the room or behind the member of the audience asking the question won't hear a thing. Always repeat the question or comment, it's good manners.

Don't ignore distractions

Lots of speakers try to pretend they don't hear or see distractions – this is a disaster. Your audience will be wondering what's wrong with you. If a pink-spotted dog runs into the room carrying a trophy in its mouth, the audience will see it and be concerned with or focus on it until you recognize it. As soon as you say, "Well, look at that ... a pink-spotted dog with a trophy," the audience will sigh in relief and concentrate on you again.

I saw a classic example of this in Hawaii. Next to the speaker's platform a plant swayed in the breeze, then fell over with a crash.

The speaker, fearing it would be a major distraction, pretended he didn't see or hear it. The audience stared at the exposed roots and the dirt for the duration of his speech. Five years later at a church meeting not far away the very same thing happened. A palm in a vase at the front of the pulpit fell over. The speaker stopped, and surveyed the damage with the audience for long enough to have everyone back looking at him. Then he shook his head slowly and said, "I should have expected that ... my competition said I was full of hot air." The audience roared and loved him for taking the blame. His acknowledgement was as effective as if he'd cleaned up the mess!

Emergency! What to do when something goes wrong in the audience

All our lives our parents, teachers, policemen, coaches, professors, etc. have always been there to tell us **what, when, how** and **if** an emergency occurred. We only had to stand by because someone was there to handle things. With speaking comes this responsibility. The minute you open your address, you have a community in your charge. Respond responsibly.

The Emergency

Twice in one year, right at the climax of my presentation, a member of my audience had an epileptic fit. Something like this is **your** *problem, because as the speaker you're the leader – which psychologically puts you in control of everything going on – including when someone chokes, faints, gets injured, has a heart attack, etc. The audience will just sit there like a bunch of helpless sheep. You're going to have to do something. Either*

1. Quickly call for and delegate the situation to the host. Since hosts are local and familiar with everything and everyone in the area, they're the ones who should call for an ambulance, etc. If not, you'll have to direct things and quickly pick and ask an individual to make the call. Or

2. Jump down off the stage and take over.

In some way you'll have to handle the situation, because when you control an audience you act for them. Remember that those close by know what's going on, but the other 95% are all instantly inquisitive. "What is it ... what ... who ...?" Get down there and help and then when things are under control, let the audience know – announce how the affected person is doing. Once the person is taken care of or carried off, you'll want to say something like: "It seems one of our friends has had a seizure (or been taken ill or whatever). He is in good hands and (if appropriate: 'His friends tell me he's going to be fine.') I'll report to you again as soon as we know."

The Emergency Story

Now what do you do? The ambulance has just hauled Harry away, and you're right in the middle of your final cementing point.

You've got to recognize the emergency and not just say, "Well, where were we?" I always tell an "emergency story" with an upbeat tone and a happy ending so I can pull people back and return to the talk.

Sometimes I stand there for a minute in silence and then sigh, and in a lowered voice say, "I guess all of us, trying to make a living and raise a family and get through life today, should come to expect emergencies and accidents once in a while. But you're probably like me and never get used to them. As a parent of six rough-and-tumble kids and a scout leader responsible for over a hundred teenagers at a time, I have never run out of them. I remember ..." Then I tell a story.

Keep control of the audience

I was doing a seminar for four hundred people once, and in the front row, about ten feet from me, was a woman with a six-month-old baby. It was a beautiful baby who didn't utter a peep, but in his little hand he had a rattle that echoed through my microphone like a threshing machine when he beat on the floor. It distracted me terribly and then I saw twenty or so members of my audience wrinkle their brow in that direction. I gave the woman a warning glance and she gave me a simple "isn't my baby cute" look back. When I saw several more people crane their necks to spot the noise, I turned to the woman and in my full speaker's authority said, "Would you mind holding that rattle, please? It's distracting the audience and me." Then I waited long enough for her to do it, and thanked her. The audience smiled approvingly and we went on.

> *You want to keep control of things not only for your own benefit, but for the audience. They'll respect you if you look after them.*

Coughers

Constant coughing by someone in the audience is another real potential distraction. The best thing is to ask someone to get them a glass of water. The water or the hint will stop the cough or make the person think about going outside or to the back of the auditorium.

Pen clickers and gum poppers

About every tenth speech I give, there's a non-stop pen clicker in the front row keeping rhythm to

something with their pen – this isn't only unsettling or irritating, it can be picked up on your mike and broadcast. You can't quite say, "Hey you inconsiderate idiot, cut out the noise," but you need to do something. Maybe ask, "Is someone clicking a pen/chewing gum? It's picking up on the mike. Ahhh, thank you, someone."

Snap, snap, flash – the picture-takers

Because they carry an expensive-looking camera, we often fail to ask people to abide by even the most elementary good manners. Too many people consider their 35mm camera permission to be obnoxious. They'll walk up in front of anyone at any point in your speech and snap, snap, snap, flash, change angles and flash again. If their camera has a motor drive they think that's a permit to blot out the view of others.

I'm amazed at the nerve of most photographers, they'll rear up in the middle of the audience, or tramp their way to the front, not once or twice, but over and over. Again, you have to control this. No one can concentrate on you or your message with camera noise and flashing lights everywhere. One flash merits a dirty look, any more and you ought to stop and embarrass the offender back to their seat. Tell photographers to stay away from the front during your speech. They can (1) use a telephoto lens from the back, or (2) take exactly the same picture before or after – simulated or re-created if necessary – and not bother the audience. Tell them you'll do exotic poses afterwards, not in the audience's time.

What about the audience with a big age span?

If an audience ranges from six to sixty years old, you'll find it tough adapting your subject matter to the span. If you have an age span, address the youngest. Always speak to the young ones, entertain and teach on the level of the youngest. No one, not even the greatest intellect, ever gets past the appeal of the childlike – we maintain our childlike mentality deep inside and we secretly love it. The most important principles are basic anyway. Uncomplicating them to a child's level is the most effective way to teach.

I was once assigned to talk at a Christmas presentation about some adult title like "How Society Profits from Jesus' Life." The audience was mainly adults, but crammed in the choir section at the back there were sixty-eight kids, their necks craning in all directions trying to find out where their parents were sitting and what was going on. Cockeyed halos were poking fellow angels in the eye, Joseph looked like a juvenile Hell's Angel in a bathrobe and the Virgin Mary's lipstick by now had migrated to her left ear. No one heard the first three speakers as they read bible stories and poems and told about the first Christmas. The kids couldn't hear or see or understand. And the adults were so terrified watching their little cloaked men beat the innkeeper with their staffs, they didn't hear either. I was the last speaker and things were at a low point. I simply walked up to and talked to and laughed with the kids before I started, and like magic, they all listened along with the adults. It was easy.

Talk down, not up, to mixed-age groups. And remember that we all like to be included in what's going on, we all like to be part of the action.

Reviving numb audiences

When water stands on top of baked soil and just evaporates (like your speech will), farmers run over it quickly with a cultivator and loosen and break up the soil so it can absorb the water. You have to do that with an audience, too.

Let's take it from the beginning. You're one of five speakers giving a presentation one morning, yours being right before lunch. The audience had a break forty minutes ago which has worn off by now, and they're all in a holding pattern waiting for lunch and the lavatory. They then introduce you and your subject, "The History of the Modern Broom." Just remember these three methods:

1. Get the audience moving: You've seen and experienced the relief of getting a chance to stand up and stretch, and you generally like the speaker who demands that you do. In this case, for example, you could ask the audience to act as if they're using different kinds of brooms. This will not only wake them up, but plant some idea of what's coming. Get them to "sweep" and push and whisk a bit and then let them sit down.

2. Get their attention: That's easily done by saying "This presentation is going to require some volunteers...." Fear will instantly grip every person in the audience. "Maybe," they'll think, "he is going to call on me!" Trying to think of an excuse or a way out will shake them up. You can probably think of forty other ways to challenge, involve, or even "threaten" them with your presentation so their adrenaline will start flowing.

3. Rewards: If anyone thinks they're going to get something at the end of or during your presentation, they'll stay awake for it. "I'm going to give a couple of these new Rubbermaid commercial brooms to the most deserving person in the audience." Let them wonder who is the most likely. Rewards are the biggest incentive going these days.

The no smoking rule

The old days of being timid about restricting smoking are over. Most audiences despise being cooped up with a smoker and especially resent having to sit by one. In a contained room, tobacco smoke will make people ill, and totally detract from a presentation. Trying to speak through a haze of smoke or to someone who is internally angry with the environment doesn't do much for your message. As the person of the hour, you are in control and all it takes is a simple request to the host that smoking not be allowed, or if smoking is a firmly established custom, that smoking be restricted to a lounge or other outside area.

- *Ask the host to separate the puffers and the purists*
- *If no one's looking, you can simply remove all the ash trays*

The drinking audience

I was hired once to speak at a large business award dinner. A lot of important people were there, with their wives in elaborate dresses. Dinner was to be at 6:30 p.m. and I was to speak one hour later at exactly 7:30. People started to arrive at 5:00 o'clock, and of course the bar was open and they drank and socialized until 6:45. Then a large dinner was slowly served and one of the big lodge owners gave complimentary wine to every table. Most people by then had had quite a few drinks as well as that heavy meal (and who knows what they drank before getting to the event). After the dinner came one hour of drawn-out award-giving and accepting, covering every assistant on thirty committees. When they handed over to me at 9:15 most of the audience was in a stupor. I could have brought a three thousand year old mummy back to life and no one would have blinked. It was one of my best, most powerful subjects and deliveries, but it went right down the drain. Whenever this happens to me I feel bad about collecting the speaking money. I now pre-assess and refuse most speaking engagements where I can't control the drinking and the time situation, or if I do accept I insist on an immediate start after dinner and get them to do any prize drawings or award-giving before or during the meal.

When you have to address a hostile audience

Audiences have their own responsibilities, the first of which is to give the speaker a chance. As a speaker, you'll get what you demand. If you're in control and command respect, you'll get it. If one or two hecklers in the audience insult me, I'll ask the host to do something or hand the audience over to him. If there are no positive results, I don't feel uncomfortable about leaving. Speaking to a hostile audience has no

and we mean that _most_ sincerely...

value that I can think of – if they aren't listening, they aren't gaining anything.

In other situations, when dealing with irate parents at a school board meeting, for instance, I let the aggressive people come up with their own answers. Often their frustration is fed by their fear that there is no better answer. Turning the tables lets them work through their feelings and very likely reach the same conclusion as you. Sometimes you'll be surprised when they do have a good solution, then it's your turn to reassess and change your position. Either way, you both benefit.

Delivery of a message while you're speaking

When hundreds of people are in one place for a few hours, something is bound to happen somewhere. Either "The lights are on in the green Ford, number 76543," or "Mr. and Mrs. Pakem ... you have an emergency at ..." or, "There is a lost set of keys," or even , "George, never mind bringing home the celery, I found some in the bottom of the refrigerator. It was going rotten but I scraped it off."

These are messages that someone feels can't wait until you sit down, and often if they don't just go through the audience hunting for the right person, they'll "Pssst" and hand the note to you. The second this is done, everyone in the room is paranoid, especially at a convention (the house or office is on fire; it's one of my kids, I just know it; I'm overdrawn at the bank and they've caught me). If you don't handle a note right away, it will throw the audience off track.

• If it's an emergency you don't need to convey it in a hoarse whisper or yell out "emergency!" Just read the name of the person, "Are you here? Good. There's a number here – someone would like you to call right away." Hand it to them and get on with the speech.

• If the message is not serious, use it as frosting in your speech. Read it and smile and say, "Well, guess who left their lights on?" The audience will love it because they're all included as a possible subject. Then read the car number and ask who the owner is.

• Have some fun with light messages, it means you and only you are keeping control of the audience and situation, whereas poor delivery of a message will take control away from you. An audience needs to know and care, but not take on the worry of something they can do nothing about.

Audience participation – be careful

No matter who or what it is, I resent being instructed as a member of an audience to "perform," especially when it involves other members of the audience. Most of us feel OK raising hands, standing up or sitting down or even answering a question, but when I'm told to clasp hands or exchange something with someone, squeeze them or hug them, tell them good morning (or the like) or repeat something silly I don't want to say, **I don't like it**. Not many people do. Some speakers seem to be always calling for this sort of thing. And it can cost them credibility. As a speaker you have the right to entreat, to urge, to offer, to suggest, but not to actually direct the actions of the people you're speaking to, that is their own free choice. One speaker asked the audience to give God a round of applause, and to tell the person next to you that

you loved them – that turned me and everyone else off. But like sheep most of them did it. Let your audience be the individuals they are and make their own decisions. If you need an active participant, ask for volunteers.

Volunteers

You still want to be careful here, though – this can be dynamite either way! If the volunteer shines, all the audience shines because he or she represents them. If the volunteer lets you down (and they often do), the audience feels they let you down and feels awkward and embarrassed. Sometimes you get people who won't talk for anything, or those who

think they have the right to take over the show and you can't shut them up. Often a volunteer (by doing too much or too little) will break the flow or spirit of your delivery by answering wrong, taking too long to do something,

101

not understanding what you want them to do, etc.

If I need to use a few volunteers, I cheat! I always ask the host or hostess to suggest a few people who are well liked and responsible and safe to use. I then make a written list and file what they look like in my mind (what clothes they're wearing, etc.), and when I ask for volunteers I inevitably point to the person or persons I selected earlier.

Don't cheat your audience of the chance to applaud

Applause has to be a spontaneous reaction. If you set it up and wait for it, you won't be popular for very long. On the other hand, if they do want to say thanks, give them a chance. A professional actor watching one of my performances gently criticized my high-speed delivery "That audience is dying to clap for you, but you move too fast from point to point and they don't have time or a place to clap – and they don't dare laugh too long or they might miss something!" At my next engagement I noticed a couple of places where people did seem to want to clap, so I paused (an unusual thing for me) and the place broke out in tremendous applause and cheers. I couldn't believe I'd been cheating them of this chance. Letting the audience respond to you with applause and laughter is important and it enhances your relationship with them.

Don't love 'em and leave 'em

After your speech, stay around until the session is over. Speakers who show up right on time and leave right at the conclusion of their speech are saying "You don't merit any more of my interest." Be visible before, during and after your presentation.

I saw a president of a university come to speak at a small ethnic group gathering, and he raved about and praised the group. Then, instead of sitting down and listening to the closing thirty minutes, he hurried off to the coffee shop. His message was dead. If you are enough a part of a group to speak and have their interest in you, then sacrifice a little time and lend an ear to them at least during the whole of your session.

Handling fans afterwards

Being patted, clawed or handshook to death, or carried out on the shoulders of an overzealous crowd is a part of your presentation – so allow a time for it. If you were a good speaker, you inspired and stimulated an audience to want more, so you can expect a fairly long aftermath. The most intense hangers-on will keep you for hours – just try to enjoy it. And you have to be prepared for the insensitive person who wants to tell you his whole life story while thirty others who've purchased books are waiting for them to be autographed. I've finally learned to handle the after-crowd the same as the audience – when I'm asked a question, I answer to the whole group, including them in the single person's problem. They like it and at least gain something from it.

What about enthusiastic admirers of the opposite sex?

As a public speaker, you are instantly a public figure, so everything you do, or someone does to you, is noticed and magnified by imagination out of all proportion. As tempting as it might be to touch, hug or in any way display physical affection to any of those in a crowd, it's a risk – don't even joke about it. I've had a beautiful woman confront me after a speech, one of my books in her hand, and a tear in her eye, saying "Don, you've been one of the biggest influences in my life.... I love you...." I feel deeply appreciated and moved and would love to enjoy a deeply and genuinely felt embrace, but never, never would

I succumb.

A woman lecturer has an equally bad risk. That gentleman in the front row whose gaze was glued on you all through your speech, or is now so intensely interested in whether you have a ride back to your hotel – the onlookers can surely see what's so obvious to you. Use the same technique as handling fans afterwards – direct any questions or comments back to the group. "Mr. Quigley has graciously offered me a lift back to the hotel. I don't need the ride but maybe someone else does?" If someone's interest is getting a little too out of hand, you must very firmly and matter-of-factly put him down. "I appreciate your enthusiasm for my talk Mr. Quigley, but I make it a practice never to spend too much time with any one member of the audience. Goodbye and good luck." You basically want to avoid any appearance of indiscretion or bad taste. That audience, for a time after you speak, is still your responsibility, and your credibility and your reputation still ride on what they think.

Rules and refresher

★ **Be in touch** – *Get eye contact with your audience, speak to them one-to-one.*

★ **Be available** – *Just for a half hour or so – nobody likes hit-and-run speakers. Give your fans a chance to express their appreciation or ask any questions they might have.*

★ **Be in charge** – *Never let the audience forget that you are running the show – think how a good teacher controls a classroom – you want to do the same.*

Chapter Ten

Special occasions and difficult situations

Not all speeches are given after dinner or during a seminar or at a conference. And not all speeches are given from a stage in a nice auditorium or in a plush hotel meeting room. There are a wide variety of situations at which you may be expected or asked to speak – perhaps only briefly, but still in a prepared, professional way. The main point to keep in mind with most of these special occasions is that **you are not the show.** You are simply part of a larger event, when the attention should be properly focused on someone else. So conduct yourself and your speech appropriately. Never, never attempt to grab the spotlight when it's not your big day. Not only is it bad-mannered and selfish, it's unprofessional. Otherwise prepare for a special occasion just as you would for any other speech, paying even more attention to your audience pre-assessment and any other specifics of length of event, time of day, size of audience, etc. The best way to be appropriate is knowing ahead of time just what kind of event you'll be fitting into.

Funerals

It's highly probable, if you've achieved anything in life, that one day the dying request of a friend will be that you be a speaker at his or her funeral. You have no choice but to accept.

There's never a "right time" for a death to occur and everyone, the family and the friends, and the aged who know they are next (they will be the biggest attenders), are emotionally numb by funeral time. Follow all the steps of preparing for a group, especially the pre-assessment of **who** will be there.

Funeral speeches, even in church, don't have to be religious. Don't feel that you're unholy if you don't rattle off a dozen scriptures and some "woes" and "yeas" and "nays." A good number of the funeral speeches and services I handled in the mission field or as the head of a congregation were not "religious."

Always arrive extremely early at the service, so that most of the people arrive after you. This will give you a feeling of familiarity and of control. Here's a basic outline I use that may give you some general guidelines as to the order of your talk:

1. Open – Immediately express your sadness – recognize how the family must feel and let them know you feel the same. Express gratitude for being there, to your friends and the family.

2. Review – Summarize your special association with the deceased. Share some close personal stories that present the deceased in a good or appealing light, express some of the deceased's most intimate wishes and joys, as you knew them. Point out that of all the things we all expect from life, the deceased got a fair share or more. (You can always think of something here that will show this to be so.)

3. Evaluate – Point out some short term and long term accomplishments of the deceased. Describe or summarize one or two specific accomplishments. Point out that the deceased left assets of family and friends and contributions to the world.

4. Counsel – Offer assistance with the adjustments the family may have to face. Provide any direction and help you can, so the family knows what to expect and where and how to get help.

5. Close – Assure the family and friends again of your sorrow, praise and thank those who came to share this moment with the family. Review the schedule (if desirable or necessary). Thank those who contributed food, etc., on behalf of the family.

Polish and formality are not nearly as necessary at a funeral as sincerity and genuine concern. I've heard "Home On The Range" sung as effectively at funerals as "How Great Thou Art." When they ask you, say **yes** – you'll come to treasure your funeral talks more than any you do – and so will your listeners.

Prayers

Many speakers coyly refer to any deity when they're speaking as "the unseen force" or the like. Take a stand, say the words God or Lord or avoid any such reference altogether.

Dos and don'ts of speaking at a funeral

There's hardly a priest or minister anywhere who can give a funeral address as well as friends or members of the family. The irreplaceable thing that *you* can do is share your ties and feelings. Too many funeral orations have a grave-digging soberness and finality that conflicts with the very faith of those attending. Enthusiasm, life, smiles, and even funny stories, can be in good taste at funerals, if they're handled correctly. Some definite "dos and don'ts" to review before you draft your final message:

Do:

• Talk to family and friends. When you prepare, remember that at times of death people need and want to talk about the deceased. Ask the family and close friends what they feel is especially important to be said or what remarks they may want to contribute. By sharing the occasion with others, the burden of being alone in the delivery will be lifted.

• Express thanks and appreciation for being asked to speak.

• Recognize the positive contribution made by the deceased to your and everyone's life.

• Let the audience know how the deceased felt about them – keep it positive.

• Make it short. Most speakers say, "Well, that won't be hard," but then they get so uptight during the preparation that they put tons of stuff in to make sure they won't run out and end up creating a risk of others dying of old age while they try to get through their talk.

Don't:

• Bury your head in books for quotes and poems. You can get a copy of the 23rd Psalm and read it with two Longfellow poems and be done with it, but this is the easy way out. Your friend asked for, and the con-gregation needs, a talk – not a poetry recital.

• Promise and predict which direction the deceased went, who they are with now. Be careful with interpreting the final judgement. He or she might have been a saint to all eyes, but a drug dealer on the sly.

• Use phrases like "for the final time," "this is the last round-up," etc. – they're trite and overused.

• Rewrite the life story. Don't try to reconstruct the person's life and heap on false praise and sanctify them. People know the good and bad of a person. Reinforce the good, whatever that is, and play down the bad, but don't exaggerate.

Weddings

You might be asked to conduct the reception or speak at weddings. Weddings are always nerve-wracking – unless you're performing the marriage, **avoid them!** Let the bride and groom get all the attention.

There's usually no place to speak at a wedding, but at the reception you may be asked to act as master of ceremonies and say a few words or introduce some guests. I've done many receptions and the only art here is to be sure to keep the bride and groom the main attraction. Stories about either or both are always appreciated, if kept short and in good taste. Keep away from wedding night jokes. If it is a fairly formal affair, then you will let the reception go on for about an hour before moving to a spot near the cake. Ask for quiet and then either propose a toast if you have been so instructed or ask for the Best Man to come forward to propose his. You may also be asked to read any telegrams or messages from people who couldn't come – once again, a little editing to keep comments within the bounds of good taste may be called for.

Master of ceremonies

This is an opportunity and a privilege, whether it's a request or an assignment. It's not only fun, it's a chance to give a lot of enjoyment to others. Take being asked to be master of ceremonies for an event as a compliment, a vote of confidence. And since you qualified for it, your job is half done already. They like you!

Now you only have to conduct the event well. You probably already have the knowledge and skill to handle almost any event, but don't underestimate what it takes to make this particular occasion work.

Remember:

> **You are not the show**
> **You are not the show**
> **You are not the show**

You're the vehicle and the grease to make it run smoothly. They have the talent, the order of events, the people, the inventory.

They have it all ready and packaged. It is your job to present the package in the most gracious manner possible.

Most people who fail as master of ceremonies do so because they're trying to provide the show themselves with their personal jokes and antics. They actually detract from the presentation and the speaker.

Here's a useful "keeping out of trouble" checklist to read before you step into the role of master of ceremonies:

● **Be totally familiar with the occasion.** Not being able to pronounce the participants' names or the title of the Concerta Contata Opus 26 D Minor is bad news. Demand a list of participants and schedule of events before the day and then review it thoroughly. If you anticipate any problem in memory or pronunciation, write the problem words or phrases on a discreet little card and take a peek before you open your mouth.

- **Don't read from a sheet of paper.** A few notes on a camouflaged card is acceptable.

- **Don't try to sell the event or appraise it after.** The event will speak for itself. People are insulted when you make judgements for them or hype them on something which might fall below expectations. And don't demand applause for unapplaudable performances.

- **Don't be eating, drinking, smoking, or carrying things when you speak.** They distract from you and the show!

- **Always be more than early.** So you can be sure nothing or nobody connected with the event is amiss.

- **Just in case.** Have five to ten minutes of your talent or someone else's ready in case there's a problem with cancellations. A standby will do a lot to relax you.

Remember: Once you assume the role of master of ceremonies you're presiding over the entire event. The stage, the sound, the organization, the temperature and the audience are all **your responsibility.**

Graduations

Be forewarned that graduation audiences are especially tough. Each person is there to see one single person – their graduate. So before and after that person appears they just aren't interested in anyone else. The audience usually comes as a family, bringing the eldest member to the youngest. An audience like this is extremely noisy and undisciplined. And they've all been provided with hand-outs to rustle and make fans and planes of.

I'm loud, short & funny — what more d'you want?

It's hard to come up with a good new way to handle a graduation ceremony. Graduation messages should be simple: "you made it." The students are interested in getting the ceremony over with and so are their teachers. And the photographers are even more obstinate and oblivious than usual – after all, each student is someone's once-in-a-lifetime photo opportunity. The formal regimented ceremony always makes administrators and students edgy and distracted and few want to listen to a speaker. I'm sure you understand what I'm implying. You won't have much going for you so don't even consider an elaborate speech along the lines of, "Now as we progress through the unknown," or a forty-name thank-you and acknowledgement list.

Make whatever you do say loud, short and funny, and design it to appeal to everyone.

Do that and you'll get their attention. If you use a visual aid or example, make it something directly related to the students or something big and familiar.

Graduation crowds like

- *Familiar stories about the students or the college*
- *Poking fun at some of their teachers*
- *Recaps of their remarkable prowess*
- *Special surprise awards to unsuspecting peers*

Graduation crowds hate

- *Bragging about school board members, principals or teachers*
- *A dry oral summary or review of the entire education process all of them have experienced*
- *Preaching: anything full of words like should, ought, better*
- *Telling them how glorious their future is*

Awards ceremonies

Award giving, if not handled right, can actually reverse the intended effect and end up a negative affair. The whole crowd should groan in admiration and appreciation, but that will only happen if an award is presented properly. Poorly done award ceremonies ruin more banquets and meetings than hecklers, interrupting waiters, and bad food. A good speaker can increase the importance of any award.

Award ceremonies, though rarely as glorious as the Oscar razzle-dazzle, are still special because there are still all-important individuals involved. Award ceremonies, however, are usually long, drawn out sessions and everyone sighs in relief when they're over. Condense all the words needed in an award ceremony by printing all the bragging on the schedule for the evening, then parade all the recipients up quickly for their hardware. Give awards fast.

If you receive an award, don't make an ass of yourself trying to recall all the anguished minutes of earning it and then kissing a total stranger. Kiss the trophy instead, show the award to everyone, take your seat and let the ceremony move on.

Panels and group discussions

One day you'll be called to be a member of a panel or group discussion. These are fun, but risky. You and five others, who thought the others would know everything and just came, will be sitting together somewhere. If one quirky, sensational or kinky thing comes out of the group, you can end up with sole responsibility for it. Watch who the groups involved are and what they're discussing. If it's highly flammable, be careful because you can get burned and it could, in turn, reflect badly on your company, your family, and your future speaking schedules.

Apart from subject cautions, the only other thing to watch is thinking you can go unprepared just because there are four or five others there. You'll end up looking dumb. If you research and come as prepared as if you were going to carry the whole thing yourself, it'll end up a real plus because when there's a bunch and one shines, it boosts you five times better than when you shine alone.

Workshops

You may find yourself called to teach what is known as a workshop. You may have to do something like three forty-five minute sessions in a row, on the same subject, in the same room, with different people coming in for each session. It's nice to only have to prepare one presentation, but by the time you get to the end of the second presentation, you may have problems remembering, "Have I already said that ... or was it the last group?" It's amazing how your three presentations will blur together and all of a sudden you mention a fact and someone says, "You've already said that." On workshops, follow your outline carefully and go by the numbers much more closely than usual.

Public debates

Don't do it unless you have to. You can be a lot better and smarter than your opponent but if he or she comes up with one stumper, even if it doesn't relate to the subject, you're done. Many of the people who listen to debates are tuned in to the negative, just watching for that one slip or weak spot. I debated for three years at college and even won some trophies at it. I highly recommend learning the formal art of argumentation (it'll serve you well in life – in business, purchasing, marriage), but to do it as a show in public, I'd forget it. If you do get squeezed into a duel, familiarize yourself well with both sides of the argument and you might come out unbroken, only bleeding.

110

Speaking outdoors

Is more difficult because nature is always a tough competitor. Rumbling trucks, droning planes, barking dogs, wind, rain, all can gang up on you. If you ever do an outside appearance (Scout awards, sports presentations, etc.), make it loud, fast, and funny and get out!

Once when I spoke to an early breakfast meeting at a coastal resort, the Chamber of Commerce had set up a nice area overlooking the bay, sheltered on a pretty section of lawn next to the resort. The meeting started at 7:30 a.m. when a continental breakfast was served. Gratitude was expressed at having someone of my magnitude (a famous toilet cleaner) in their midst and then it was over to me. By sheer physical endurance I managed to get by with a good speech, but let me share with you the "outside" things that happened during the forty-minute speech:

• The minute I stood up to speak, at 7:55, everyone in town either started or parked their car in their garages (which must have been designed like amplifiers).

• The wind came up – and the microphone responded with hissing and distortion.

• The groundsman arrived and began to trim the lawn with a power mower.

• Several of the ships and large yachts in the bay started their motors and the giant tugboats started their 88,000 horsepower diesel engines.

• All of the hotel's day projects for the kiddies began right next to me.

• Two more lawn mowers started up.

• Passers-by, hearing the laughter and seeing my toilet suitcase, stopped and crowded around.

• The pigeons made a few bomb runs.

• My papers blew off the tables and there was a mad rush to retrieve them.

Ten or twelve other minor interruptions occurred, but we won't dwell on them. Remember, speaking outside is difficult because of all the competition, and because you can't fully control the environment. Even the smoke from a campfire will (every time, guaranteed) defy nature and follow you. Think about practical matters when you prepare to speak outside. Here are the things I do to improve a bad situation:

• Make sure the sound system is as good as it possibly can be.

• Snuggle my back against something if possible that will obscure any distractions going on behind me.

• Print my notes/outline on cardboard or some other heavy material, so it won't blow away or rustle in the microphone.

• Situate the set up to keep the sun out of my eyes and the eyes of the audience.

• Use "extra hold" hair spray, so I won't have to worry about my hair being blown about.

111

When you have to speak off the cuff

One thing about being asked to speak at only three seconds notice, is that the speech is as much a surprise to the audience as it is to you, so that starts things off on an even keel. They aren't expecting anything and haven't had time to build up their expectations, so you aren't obliged to give a mammoth address.

An occasion will go something like this: "Ladies and gentlemen, before we move on, I'd like you to know that we are fortunate to have Fay Fruitceller here with us today, and we'd like to hear a few words from her. Fay, come on up here." That's it, then everyone applauds and there you are stuck with no notes, no jokes, no plot. You can either rise graciously to a situation like this with a very short remark or two: "It's great to be here with you all and experience the first twelve-foot snowdrifts of my life. I'm looking forward to getting acquainted with you and your organization ... thank you for having me." Then sit down, and they'll love it and you. Or you can comment briefly on the occasion that brings you together, or why you are there, or on something another speaker has said, etc. Or you can do what I do when attending anything, whether it's a funeral, reception, outing, or whatever, and think that there's always a chance I might be asked to speak briefly.

At least half the time, you'll feel it coming before it comes, as everyone is gathering around you and saying "Wow look who's here." So I always jot a little "old stand-by" topic or two on the back of a business card, a couple of stories about my profession or work that I know from experience will bring down the house, or a personal experience that has a very universal application. I carry the card in my wallet. Then when I'm suddenly called upon to speak, I don't have to worry about a blank mind. Right now, do that, take out a little card and fill it in and prepare for your coming (maybe 10 years away) impromptu speech. Your worries are over!

Another ace in the hole for impromptu salvation is to watch other speakers' responses in such situations, how they handle it, what they say ... people will teach you much of what is good and not good to say. I acquired many of my speech skills watching others, adopting the good and avoiding the bad!

Question and answer sessions

If you do any kind of job at all on your subject you're going to stimulate questions. And every audience has a few people with the guts to ask them out loud, so whether you like to or not, whether you're prepared or not, you'll get them sometime, somewhere.

112

Questions can endorse your credibility better than any brochure or bragging in a presentation. But a poorly or slowly asked question – or the wrong question – can kill the flow, spirit, and goal of your presentation. It can stimulate other questions further off the subject, use up time, and lead you into an area you aren't technically or emotionally prepared for.

Once a question is asked, even a poor one, you have to address it.

To give you an idea of the kinds of problems they can pose, doing a breakfast television show once, the two hosts and I really set a pace. It was without doubt the funniest, most fast-moving and informative six minute slot we'd ever done on the show. Then we took a couple of calls as was customary. An elderly woman called, and it took her thirty seconds just to ask the question (stopping the quick flow and repartee). She had a problem with her husband (she described him in some detail). His leather coat (she described it in some detail) had a silk lining and his perspiration had stained under the armpit area (she described this, too, in some detail) – what should she do? Experienced and savvy as the producers were, what station could cut off an old lady? Basically, regardless of how well I answered the question, the show was over.

If you think falling back on questions and answers is a solution to being unprepared for a presentation, you'll deserve what you get, a further loss of confidence and situations even worse than the one just described.

The biggest problem is that often a question from someone in a large group is totally individual and remote and not of the slightest interest to the rest of the group, yet requires twenty minutes to answer. This turns off all the rest of the audience and wastes everyone's time. Often, too, in groups there are some egotistical intellects who never get asked to speak or perform and a question and answer session is their big chance and they'll join in and expound and try to take the session out of your hands.

Questions are a weak way to end a presentation. Using a question and answer as the actual conclusion of a speech is a real loser

– though a lot of speakers do it. I won't! I'd stay after I conclude my speech and answer questions all night if necessary – but never in or as part of my talk. The very end of a presentation mustn't be a possibly hostile or irrelevant question. You want to talk to the finish, not leave it in the hands or lips of others.

I like to finish my presentation completely and then ask for questions, so that whatever happens it won't harm or reflect upon my presentation.

I don't want to frighten you away from questions because timely, well-handled questions can double your communication results, but remember that they're a high-risk option to be handled with caution.

Delicate subjects!

Always acknowledge that you're aware the issue exists, then drop it or take a stand, but don't skirt or straddle the issue!

Making the most of the Q & A – ten ways to control question time

You can ignore the raised hands and say, "It's in my book," or "Later," or, "Now that's a good question – I'm glad you asked that," or, "Are there any questions before moving on," etc. But these methods are weak and amateurish. The real professionals:

1. Poll the audience beforehand. If you have help, suggest that people write down questions and hand them to the host, then you can not only gauge which are the questions of more general interest, but pull the audience in in the process. The way to do this is to re-ask the question back to them and raise your hand as you ask it. "Aha – how many of you have this same problem with your pet always piddling on the same place on your carpet?" The place will generally come unglued, and you'll then answer the question.

2. Let the audience know the rules. Tell the audience in advance that there'll be a question and answer session and spell out the guidelines. Ask that they keep questions within the subject, for instance, and that they keep questions short so others can have a chance.

3. Have a plant in the audience. If you're worried about getting the session started, a little ahead of time give someone in the audience an ice-breaking question or two to ask as soon as the session opens.

4. Use a mediator. Ask your host, if necessary, to take control of the question and answer session. He or she can then be responsible for fielding the questions, keeping them short, cutting off the egomaniacs and ramblers, and leaving you the job of answering, which is, after all, what you're there for.

5. *Keep your answer short.* And answer the whole audience, not just the questioner. The main thing to avoid in a question and answer session is getting bogged down. If the questions are short and the answers are short, the session will be much more enjoyable for everyone.

6. *Beat them to it.* Ask your own questions! After I demonstrate how to use a vacuum, for example, and then tell them most vacuum attachments are worthless, I know they're all wondering how to vacuum stairs and edges if you have no attachments. So I ask, "Then how do you vacuum stairs and edges?" The whole audience gives a relieved nod and smiles, and then I answer it.

7. *Repeat the question.* If a question is asked too softly, most people won't hear it, so your brilliant answer will be unappreciated. Even if asked loudly, it's a good idea to repeat the question, in a condensed form, as a matter of habit – it's the polite thing to do, your audience will greatly appreciate it, and it keeps you in control and dominant.

8. *Maintain momentum.* If you get a tough, embarrassing, or time-consuming question, have a pat answer for it, like: "I appreciate that question, and I've had it before. If you want a complete answer this is not the time or place to handle it, but I'll be happy to meet you after we finish. Anyone interested in the answer is also welcome."

9. *Turn it back to them if you have to.* If you do get a difficult or putting-you-on-the-spot question that you can't wriggle out of or postpone ask, "Would you explain that again and tell me the reason you ask that?" While trying to define it the questioner will, in most cases, give you some straws to grip or end up answering his or her own question or talk him or herself out of it, or at least take the zing out of it. There are times when a rude question deserves a somewhat rude answer, "Exciting as it may be, sir, my private life (or business life or principles, etc.) are personal information and concern no one else."

10. *Admit you don't know everything.* People hate infallibility in others. If you don't know the answer say, "That situation has never really come up. Are there any of you out there (listening in or in the audience) that can help me answer this one?" This is a great way to handle an "I don't know" question. What you have cleverly done is make the audience an expert by asking them for help. And they'll think you're even smarter for going to them.

Chapter Eleven

You're on the air: radio and television speaking

Radio and television intimidate a lot of people but they shouldn't. Most media speaking is fun and easy. Your host is almost always professional enough to guide you and make even an amateur look good. If you are prepared and know your stuff, talking on radio and appearing on television will become some of the most enjoyable experiences of your speaking career. The key here is being relaxed – and if you're prepared you have nothing to get uptight about – and letting your host or hostess do most of the work. If you follow your host's lead and direct your comments and talk to him or her you won't go wrong.

Radio phone interviews

These are simple and effective. You'll get to do some in your life if you're lucky. I've done more than five hundred, some taped, but mostly live broadcasts. A phone interview is nothing more than you on a phone (anywhere) talking to a radio or TV station or newspaper somewhere else. I've done them from Idaho to New Zealand, Hawaii to Canada, Alaska to Manchester. They connect your phone signal into their broadcasting equipment, and you just talk normally, sitting in your chair. They'll make sure the line is good and will always call you or call you back so that any costs go to them. I always have a notebook or pad on which I write

Ssh! Mommy's working!

the names and where I'll be speaking to so I don't forget to call. This will also make sure that you get names and places right – and remember to have the phone numbers too, in case you're cut off.

I'm as comfortable as a kid at

an ice cream counter when I'm interviewed by phone because just like all that ice cream laid out on display, I also have in front of me all sorts of information – jotted down ideas, extra stories, and some of my best hooks to get listeners to phone in. And I have a thick pad of paper right beside me so that I can write down the name of every person who phones, then I can address them by name or refer back to them if I need to. It's easy and fun, and there's no way you can forget what to say.

● **Extension tension** – Don't forget, this is one time that a million people might be listening in on your call so make sure everyone in the office or house knows you're "doing an interview." My wife picked up the phone during a big radio interview once and hollered, "Come and get it, honey!"

● **Find a quiet place** (phone booths are suicidal) – I was in the lobby of a BBC station in London when the largest station in Belfast, Northern Ireland called and wanted a live interview right then. Rock music was blaring over the lobby loudspeaker, four people were getting directions from the receptionist, and the host on the Irish show not only had a very hard accent to follow but he was assisted by two other Irish locals whose accents were even more exotic. The guests sitting in the studio (whom he quickly included in the activities) could barely hear, and everyone there was shooting questions at me. Situations like these shouldn't be allowed to occur, because there's just no way you can give a decent performance. In a phone-in interview, the public calls the station and then the station patches you and the caller together, so now you have the clarity of two lines to worry about. If you can't hear, don't fake it, tell the host, "John, I can't hear our caller." He'll repeat the question or comment and then you can respond.

Media people are sharp, and they do enough worrying for both of you. They'll make sure you have a good line and tell you all you need to know. Just be sure to write the host or hostess's name down so you don't call Jim "Harry" or Sue "Mary."

Taped interviews

Before you begin, ask what day and time the interview will be transmitted so you won't say "good morning" to an audience who's listening to you at 10:30 in the evening, and so you won't comment on the beautiful weather today (when you record) and they're transmitting it during a typhoon.

Because I do hundreds of different interviews a year (and you will do many in your life), here's a copy of the form I use to guide me and my office to acquiring the necessary information to do a good job. Here, too, you want to follow up and keep a record. You'll find it very useful in the future.

INTERVIEW

Date: _____ / _____ / _____   Time: _____ a.m.
p.m.

Length of Interview: _____

Show: _____

_____
name

_____
address

☐ **Radio**   ☐ **LIVE**
☐ **TV**   ☐ **TAPED**
☐ **Newspaper**
☐ **Magazine**

Phone: _____   _____
Office   Home/Emergency

Contact: _____   *Host:* _____

Interview on: _____   Circulation: _____

_____

_____   Response to Interview: _____

Offer: _____   _____

_____   _____

_____   _____

Notes/Requests: _____

_____

_____

_____

_____

_____

_____

_____

_____

Subject Covered: _____   Evaluation: _____

_____   _____

_____   _____

"Speaking" over the phone

If you can't be there to speak to a group, you can phone in and amplify it. Marvin Klein, a cleaning supplies manufacturer, runs several training and motivational seminars every year in Chicago, and he likes me to give those attending a Don Aslett shot-in-the-arm and I always do. Whether I'm in England, Idaho, Alaska, or Florida, we just plan the time, one of us phones and the call is switched onto the speaker phone. I can hear the group and they can hear me. When and if you do one of these, just forget the phone is in your hand and lay into the crowd. Of course, have three or four minutes of what you want to say outlined. It can just be a humorous report on what you're doing, what you've done recently, and what's coming down the road. You might call this a broadcast greeting or short hello speech. The value is making contact with someone at an important moment, at very little or no cost. On a pre-arranged call, before you talk to the entire group, ask the client if there's anyone you know in the crowd and then when you get on, greet that person – it works like magic. These little talks are very enjoyable and effective and cost nothing except the phone time.

Appearing on television

Everyone who does TV always comes out of the experience saying "Wow, that wasn't a bit hard." And it isn't. Don't think for a moment that a station is going to let you do a bad job. TV people have to do their thing every day, under all sorts of pressures of time and technology and they've dealt with many an inexperienced person before, and like a good and wise parent, they'll take care of you and if you have even half a wit they'll not only make you look good, but see that you enjoy yourself while you're doing it.

I've done hundreds of TV appearances now, including a number of national shows. The basic format is pretty much the same for them all, and they have someone to help you and make your job easier. (You may be asked to sign a release for any interview by the media.)

For TV appearances you don't do anything different than what you've already learned. The secret of a successful TV appearance is to be natural and normal and let the host guide you. If you go blank or can't answer a call or question, they'll do it for you, so gracefully that the audience will think you did it. TV people are sharp, they can handle under-talkers and over-talkers smoothly, and there are only two big things to remember:

1. The time slots for TV and radio are short, so you can't tell the *full* story of grandmother's secret recipe.

2. They might put make-up on you.

Make your plans known

Remember, you know more about your work, yourself, and your subject than anyone in the world, including all of the people at the studio. So go ahead and outline and plan for what you think you do best, for what has worked before, and try to include your best visuals, and some of the questions that you know will stimulate the viewers. You are the best person to establish the theme and "script" of your appearance, so don't be afraid to suggest it.

Send a copy of your outlined plan to the producer and the host beforehand and they'll literally hug you for it. Tell them what you like to do and can do well, and what props you'll bring. They're professionals and will help you work it out beautifully.

A floor director will tell you how to hold up your visual aids (one of the big things to remember here is to hold it still), and which camera is picking them up. You don't have to worry about sound (voice level), your visibility, getting rid of distractions, and the other details of normal speaking engagements because the TV people and their cameras and equipment are expert at focusing and moving around and editing what they get. They will tell you whether the show is being taped to be shown later or live. I used to like taping because if you scratched under your arm, or bit your lip, they could erase it, but now I enjoy appearing live.

Host cards

As with other speaking, you want to be sure you know your stuff before you go on. The hosts will generally have outlined questions for you beforehand. Here is a host card used for one of my appearances and one used on Gary Crosby two months before me:

As you can see by these examples, if your subject is controversial, you'd better be ready to answer some pointed questions.

Gary Crosby   Monday, April 4

MENTION: He is the author of "GOING MY OWN WAY"

QUESTIONS: 1. What was your purpose in writing your book?
            2. This book is being called "Daddy Dearest" by some because of your accounts of mental and physical cruelty by your father. How do you feel about that label?
            3. Because of your father's relatively untarnished image, many of your revelations have come as a shock to many of his fans. Why had there been no indication of this part of his life before?
            4. What has been the reaction so far from other family members?
            5. If Bing were alive today ... how would he feel about this book?

Don Aslett   Thursday, June 7

MENTION: He is the author of "CLUTTER'S LAST STAND"

TOPIC: How to de-junk your life and get rid of things you really don't need.

QUESTIONS: 1. How do you judge junk?
            2. What are some common excuses for holding onto clutter?
            3. Who are the biggest junk-savers, men or women?
            4. How do you handle junky gifts that you'd rather not keep around the house?
            5. People collect a lot of souvenirs when they're away. Does most of that generally turn out to be junk as well?
            6. What are the most common pieces of junk that people collect?

Get to the media ... before they get to you

If the media is coming to you – to film a presentation for the local news for instance – the situation is entirely different. Unlike going to the studio, you must take control, or your presentation could be ruined. Once a national television show filmed me at a live seminar and there were nine hundred people there who paid to see it. The TV crew cared about one thing and one thing only – getting footage. It was three hours of agony. National publicity or not, I vowed never to repeat it. The media can sometimes appear to care about one thing – getting a good show for the two-minute clip they will – or might – use. If they damage your presentation in the process, that's your problem. So ...

● **State your policy** *on recordings and pictures before you commit yourself to speak and put the burden of media control and limitation on your host.*

● **Arrange for pictures or interviews before or after your presentation.** *I make it a policy to do face-to-face interviews and to be available for photographs either before or after my speech and the media and photographers, etc. all accept this if they get the message that you are in control.*

● **Let the audience know what's happening.** *If there is going to be filming during your presentation, tell your audience something like, "You all watch important things on TV at home? Well, you're going to see where it comes from. The local TV station wanted to cover our event and will be shooting some of us, so relax. If they get a bad shot of you they'll edit it out." Then everyone will be aware of the cameras and less bothered.*

● **Carry a little media kit.** *Just a folder with a good black-and-white photo of you, a brochure, a few press releases, a few excerpts from your book or articles, customer testimonials, an introduction card – whatever best applies to you and your subject, and hand it to journalists and reporters.*

● **Don't talk off the record.** *If you don't want to see it in print, don't say it. It's always possible that a journalist will disregard a request for confidentiality and print whatever he sees fit, or he may forget what's been told off the record and what hasn't. Either way, you may find your "for background information only" comments in print – and have to live with them.*

● **Be quotable.** *Answer questions directly and briefly; the journalist wants an answer, not a monologue. Avoid clichés and little-known industry jargon. Phrase your answers posivitely, actively in words and ways that are interesting.*

Rules and refresher for TV

- Dress appropriately – remember stripes and whites strobe and glare – dress simply and conservatively.
- Know what the questions will be.
- Tell the host what you can and want to do.
- Have visuals.
- Be early – you'll get more time with the host.
- Don't confuse names (Jack/Jim/Carol/Carolyn). And especially remember the host's and hostess's name.
- Keep alert – don't turn up with coffee jitters or in a cigarette or chemical haze.
- Don't sit in a swivel chair.
- Keep records – what you did, with whom, how the time was used.
- Make a copy of your appearance. If you bring your own blank ¾" tape, the station will generally dub you a copy of your appearance. Or get a friend to make a copy at home. If necessary some towns have taping agents who can also do you a copy.

Chapter Twelve

The professional game

The great majority of speeches and addresses are given for free. Most of yours will probably be free, too, at least in the beginning. I gave my first two thousand speeches and presentations for free. I even paid my own expenses. Free speakers get lots of experience and get better and better and finally one day, someone will offer to pay you a fee. Getting money for talking is pretty phenomenal when you think about it, especially if you enjoy it. My first speeches were for the scouts, community groups, schools, local clubs and churches. Good, free speakers get popular fast. This is because many organizations will cheerfully pay for the service and the coffee but never consider paying the speaker. Today, five thousand speeches and presentations later, I get paid to speak all over the world. I get paid for travel expenses, food, extras and a fee for the speech itself. And five thousand speeches later I still give lots of free speeches to scouts, community groups, schools, clubs, and churches.

Setting your rates

Because fees and expenses for speaking are something I and other speakers are constantly asked about, I'll try to give you a framework for setting your rates.

Don't get overwhelmed by the Big Leaguers. The "speaker bureau" greats, the professionals. In most cases it isn't their speaking they're in demand for, it's their media-created image and celebrity status, and the attendance they can draw to an event. They're often not the best or even the good speakers of the world, but athletics, politics, or entertainment has made them highly visible and, of course, anything and everything about them is marketable.

Even a dry, know-nothing address can earn them a fortune and they often aren't as good as you. I spoke at a presentation with two of America's greatest newsmen/columnists. They got $15,000 each and I got $1,500. Yet I outrated them in audience evaluations and my tape outsold one of theirs by 5 to 1.

There is no official table of

speech charges. Everyone gets what they can, when and where they can, and rates and values vary with how good you are, what field you're in, and how many people have heard of you. I've seen real professionals who can command a high fee to speak do it free or take just a small fee because they like the people involved or the cause. My speaking fee varies from free all the way up to a lot, and there's not a few I've refused at high fees because I don't believe in the cause or the principles of the parties asking me. Only you and the people hiring or asking you know how good you are and how much you're worth.

Know your worth

Hired tongues are like hired guns. Your reputation, results, and fame determine your worth – learn it. What the market can afford to pay means a lot, too. One TV host I met, who also does speaking and

seminars, said she got lots of work at $1,500 a session, when she increased it to $2,500 she got none. Consider all these things and set your own fee, and don't be afraid to do a few free for the experience (and a lot still free later to keep sharp).

The going rate

• *Most conventions/groups have a $300-$500 (£150-£300) budget for the small or immediate speaker to do a session. This is also about the amount small local companies pay for a local talk with few hand-outs from a good speaker.*

• *If you're one of the main speakers and it's a large, expensive occasion, they'll usually allow $750-$2,000 (£400-£1100).*

• *If you're well-known and the star of the occasion, doing the main address or seminar, it'll generally go from $3,000-$7,000 (£1,700-£4,000). If you become a national superstar giving speeches and talks everywhere you could go from $10,000 to $25,000 (£5,500-£15,000) an appearance.*

I would like to warn you about doing too much for free or waiving your fee because you "get so much exposure." Most promises of side benefits and spin-offs from free appearances seldom materialize. The organizers of one big freebie I did said fifteen thousand people would be there and that I'd sell a thousand books, and that sounded

The right price: five rules for charging

Rule No. 1 – Anybody asking you to speak professionally should at least pay all of your travel and other expenses. Most of them know that and will tell you so. If they don't, be sure to mention it, because it's pretty embarrassing trying to claim for a plane ticket after the event, by which time the company or group thinks it was a privilege for you to get to speak to them.

Rule No. 2 – When someone calls they'll generally ask you, "What is your fee?" A lot of people asked this question are caught off guard and stutter and stammer and that is not very impressive. Have your fee or charge ready and tell them. It's your place to do so, and if they don't like it, you'll hear a groan or silence. Or a quick "Is that all? We thought you'd be three times that!" (In cases like this just feel silently sick and remember it for next time.)

Rule No. 3 – Always confirm the conversation by summing it up on a typed page, stating the date, time, and place of your appearance, the amount they agreed to pay for it and when it will be paid, and send them a copy and keep one in your files and take one copy along to the presentation with you. **Be sure to do this.** The fee you'll be paid, and the content of your speech, should be decided upon at least a month in advance.

Rule No. 4 – Some people and groups who are used to getting everything free might not even dream of paying a speaker and will never ask your fee. The best way to handle this is to be aggressive. At an appropriate point early in the conversation say something like: "I generally get ____ per speech or full-day appearance. Depending on what the occasion or charity is, I may lower my fee." That gives the caller some options, and a chance to decide, without being cornered.

Rule No. 5 – When my would-be hosts and I can't agree on a fee, I always apologize, let them know I regret it, and leave the hope that maybe we can work something out next time.

good to me. There were sixty people there and I sold no books.

Always ask the people paying you to be inconspicuous about it. Many times, right after I've given a free or expenses-only address to a group and am still on the platform, the organizer will push the money in my hand saying, "I know you won't want to forget this." To avoid this tactless moment arrange to have all payments, be it the travel expenses or your fee, made in total privacy!

To be professional, be organized

When your speech is over, clean up your notes and outline, type them up if necessary, and file them in a notebook along with any comments you want to record about the occasion. It'll only take a few minutes and will save you hundreds of hours of agony and future preparation. You might not and should not give exactly the same speech again, but maybe something quite similar in similar circumstances. There are some very good reasons to file, such as when:

• You get to do the same job, for the same people: If you do the job well, you'll be asked back again next year and the next or maybe sometime in the future. A good speaker doesn't give the same talk again to the same group and how can you remember what you did say or do? **Record!**

• Or the same request, in another town: You gave a phenomenal address in Oregon, and now New Mexico calls you for next year and you've already got it done! (With improvements you've made on it from your comments.)

• Strengthening your speeches: After a talk, people will often send you stories, anecdotes, and ideas for expansion of your subject. You can easily drop these into the structure of your address and have a five times better talk, at no cost.

Any time we find something that works (like the right trout fly, a rousing joke, a delectable gourmet dish), we have a natural tendency to re-use it again and again. A good speech is the same. You find a real flow once, the audience loves it and so you change it a little and re-use this basic format (often called a "circuit talk").

Giving the same speech to different groups in different areas is the normal speaker's route, because someone will hear you and say "I'd like all the schools to hear this" or "All the company branches should arrange for you to visit and speak to them." This is a great opportunity for you and it adds to your repertoire. You'll be able to add comments made at previous presentations, a few stories, etc. and your speech will improve, grow and change.

It was so good to hear that talk... again...

This can be good reliable magic that just gets better — as long as you *don't* use it on the same people. It's very embarrassing to repeat most of the same stuff you've used before to the same group. That's why I strongly encourage you to type or somehow process the outlines of your talks and file them under headings of the sponsor's address. Make a careful note of when, where, and in which town you gave your talk. Write it all out and keep a record of what you did and said. If it's a new group, you can use the same speech format. If it's the same group, review the outline of what you delivered last time and use expanded or completely new material.

How to get jobs

I've been asked many times if I belong to a national or local speaking organization. I've never wanted my name associated with a speaking group. That's a personal thing, I admit. I have a motto posted in my office that says, "Be so good, they come after us!" That, in my opinion, is the best and cheapest way to market your speaking. Just prepare and do an outstanding delivery every time and every single person there will be a full time salesman for you. You'll have more to do than you can handle. I always pass around cards or brochures to everyone attending, as all are potential friends, contributors of ideas, and future clients.

Developing a speaking policy

As every organization, game or government has a set of rules or policies that establish the boundaries they work in, so you, as a professional speaker, should adopt some criteria and standards about your speaking appearances – when, where, and what you will do as a speaker. Then when you get a request you won't have to hesitate and debate with yourself all over again when certain questions come up. My own speaking policies are quite simple:

- No paid professional speeches on Sundays.
- A map and directions must always be included in the final confirmation packet.
- I will only ever speak in non-smoking areas.
- No one else can or will try to make sales or solicitations during my presentations.
- I never sign autographs during the break.
- A complete typed record and evaluation will be kept on all talks.

Develop your own speaking policy with the rules you feel good about.

I have my "guidelines" printed on the back of my speaking confirmation form – please feel free to adapt this to your own needs.

Guidelines

As a courtesy from one professional to another, the following are some procedures I expect you to follow:

☐ **Set Up:**

I like to be at the area or place where I'm performing at least an hour beforehand so I can set up and test the sound system, visuals, etc. If another meeting is going on at that time we can leave it, but where possible I need to be in early to prepare myself and my equipment.

☐ **Introduction:**

Nothing ruins a good presentation or wastes more valuable speaking time than someone who overdoes the introduction. Enclosed is a brief pamphlet that I outlined which covers things. The blank is for special remarks.

☐ **Sound:**

Make sure that a good sound system is available and in good working order. I prefer a lavalier neck microphone, and I'll use yours if you have one. I carry a few that fit almost any system and can usually tap in.

☐ **Food Control:**

I will not speak while food is being served, eaten or cleared up. If it's a dinner I'll start when everyone has finished their meal, and I expect the service people to wait until my presentation is over to begin clearing the tables. Please keep the kitchen noise down until my presentation is completed.

☐ **Audience:**

I'd like you to be sure the audience is seated and quiet before I start. I prefer no smokers close to me on the front row or head table.

☐ **Camera/Publicity**

I'm always there early and will stay after for pictures and interviews. Allowing photographers to stand between me and the audience during my presentation, snapping pictures and flashing lights, will be extremely irritating to both of us.

☐ **Announcements:**

If you have any special announcements or thank-yous you'd like me to make, or something I can do for you to improve the event, please hand them to me and I will work them neatly into the presentation.

Well, how did you do?
Evaluating your speeches

The follow-up request and comments from the host and audience will give you an instant impression of your "grade". Your personal excitement will also be a prime indicator of just how well you really did. For the first few times ask a good friend or critic to use this little checklist.

SPEECH APPRAISAL

The listener should conscientiously complete this form
and hand it to you to study after the presentation.

SPEAKER   SUBJECT _____

Date _____

	Poor	Very weak	Weak	Fair	Adequate	Good	Very good	Excellent	Superior	
	1	2	3	4	5	6	7	8	9	Comments
1. Introduction										
2. Clarity of purpose										
3. Choice of words										
4. Bodily action-gesture-posture										
5. Eye contact & facial expression										
6. Vocal expression										
7. Desire to be understood										
8. Poise and self-control										
9. Adapting material to audience										
10. Organization of material										
11. Conclusion										

Copy some of these and get help. Your feelings might suffer for a few minutes, but I always like to see evaluations, ratings and comments on my presentations so I can repeat what I had success with and avoid using the losers again.

You should always keep a record of the evaluations and appraisals of your presentations. The mark of a professional in any field is to be humble and able to ask for and accept criticism. Some of the best singers still take singing lessons.

If you or others have made recordings of your speeches, these can be helpful in analyzing your progress. You'll want to run out of the room the first few times you listen to one of these, and you're going to make some surprising discoveries, but they'll grow on you after a while, and will become a useful tool of self-evaluation.

When they change the date of a convention that 5,000 people are attending so they can get you as a speaker, then you'll know you've made it. And it will happen, if you just bring out that speech that's inside you!

Index

Have you read these othe

Is There Life After Housework?

Don Aslett's complete cleaning guide tells you how the professionals do it so you can save up to 75% of the time you spend on housework. In this boo you'll find specific, step-by-step instruction on how to clean every area of your home, including ...
- the right kind of tools and equipment for the job
- how to pick up dust quickly — the first time around
- how to keep your bathroom sparkling in just 3-1/2 minutes a day
- dozens of ways to prevent housework

Housework is necessary, but with Don Aslett's approach, you'll discover that there really is life after housework!
192 pages/Illustrated/$8.95, paper

Do I Dust or Vacuum First?

This book offers quick, easy-to-apply answers to 100 of the toughest, most-often-asked questions about housecleaning. Questions that people like **you** ask Don Aslett in his frequent housecleaning seminars across the country. For example:
- How often should I clean my drapes?
- Why can't I get my sponge mop clean?
- How do you keep dirt paths out of your carpet?
- Is it cheaper and better to make your own cleaners?

The answers to these questions (and 96 others) are all here. Practical, inexpensive ways to make your house shine, and in about half the time!
183 pages/Illustrated/$7.95, paper

Clutter's Last Stand

Through anecdotes, charts, cartoons, quizzes, and "bumper snickers," Aslett humorously delves into the full range of junk areas (home, car, office, wardrobe ... even friendships) pinpointing problem areas and offering practical ideas for getting rid of unnecessary clutter and cutting it off at its source.

For all who have waged war on clutter and lost, here is the inspiration to get the job done once and for all!
276 pages/Illustrated/$9.95, paper

Who Says It's a Woman's Job to Clean?

Somewhere it started ... that it's a woman's job to clean. It became a tradi- tion ... even an institution ... and is still with us today. The purpose of this book is to dispel that old myth and get with the times. Aslett lists all the standard excuses—and demolishes them one at a time. He then proceeds to give men a crash course on cleaning. This book is fun, practical, and essen- tial reading for men (and women!) everywhere!
112 pages/Illustrated/$5.95, paper

oks by Don Aslett?

et Clean-Up Made Easy

Don Aslett deserves a doggone standing ovation! This book not only tells ou how to clean up every pet mess imaginable, but also how to "petproof" our home to prevent accidents from occurring! A **must** for pet lovers verywhere!

44 pages/Illustrated/$8.95, paper

Make Your House Do the Housework

vith Laura Aslett Simons

In this book, Don Aslett shares hundreds of practical, exciting ways to edecorate, remodel, design, or build cleaning and maintenance out of your nome, including floor coverings, exterior finishes, and window treatments, ust to name a few!

208 pages/Illustrated/$11.95, paper